ENGLISH ROMANTIC PARTSONGS

Selected and edited by

Paul Hillier

Contents

Introduction

There are many misinformed opinions about nineteenth-century England, but some of the more regrettable ones concern music, where the use of the word 'Victorian' is still usually pejorative. In most cases any such opinion is a received one—relatively few people have actually listened to more than a few fragments of 'Victoriana', though the tendency to ridicule the style and much that its period apparently represents may seem natural to anyone performing it today. Yet if the practice of 'early music' teaches us one thing, it should be to approach the music of the past on its own terms and with reference to the cultural climate that nurtured it; that done, we may treat it simply as music to satisfy our own tastes and needs. It would not be out of place to suggest that Victorian music is now due for a revival—on its own terms—and that *we* would be the benefactors of such consideration. We would at the very least become more fully aware of our musical heritage and of how things today came to be as they are.

It is a common assumption that the rediscovery of 'early' music and the growth of societies for singing madrigals were a development of the early twentieth century, to which latterly we have added professionalism and a greatly extended repertoire as the result of exhaustive research. In fact this began in the eighteenth century (in truth it had never entirely stopped). In 1741 an amateur countertenor by the name of John Immyns, an attorney by profession, founded the Madrigal Society and

> got together a few persons who had spent their lives in the practice of psalmody . . . They were mostly mechanics; some weavers from Spitalfields, others of various trades and occupations; they met at first at the Twelve Bells, an alehouse in Bride-Lane, Fleet-Street, and Immyns was both their president and instructor; their subscription was five shillings and six-pence a quarter, which defrayed their expenses in books and music paper, and afforded them the refreshments of porter and tobacco . . .
>
> (Hawkins, *A General History . . . of Music,* London, 1776)

Nor was this the oldest musical club. Immyns's taste for 'ancient' music had no doubt been acquired through his work as copyist for Dr Pepusch's 'Academy of Ancient Music', and its activities and success were stimulated by the general interest in antiquarian pursuits that accompanied the growth of romanticism and formed a reaction to the increasing industrialization of town and country. The immediate result of such societies was an expansion of the publication of old music, which soon ranged back to the later Middle Ages, but in time the composition of new repertoire was also encouraged. In 1811 the Madrigal Society inaugurated a competition for new madrigals for which Samuel Wesley composed *O sing unto mie Roundelaie.* Although it did not win, it is a fine example of successful pastiche, complete with antiquarian spelling in its original printing.

Composition in imitation of the madrigal style continued throughout the nineteenth century; there are examples by William Beale, T. F. Walmisley, John Stainer, and Charles Wood, to name only a few. But the most significant figure in the madrigal revival, and one of England's more gifted nineteenth-century composers, was Robert Lucas Pearsall.

Pearsall was born in Bristol and studied law, though ill health cut short his career. He turned instead to music and other largely antiquarian interests, and was a founder member of the Bristol Madrigal Society (1837). He later settled abroad and purchased a castle on the shores of Lake Constance, a suitable setting for his various medieval hobbies. His partsongs, including many madrigalian compositions, form a modest but significant contribution to the English music of the period. Indeed, works such as *Lay a garland* have been paid lip-service for decades, but are still almost unknown to modern audiences. In order to stimulate some interest in an unjustly neglected minor composer one sometimes risks exaggerating his praise: Pearsall's music is often extremely attractive and in some instances deeply expressive—no more, no less, but he certainly merits our attention.

The madrigal is distinguished from the partsong by its polyphonic part-writing and generally non-chromatic harmony. The partsong itself is more harmonically conceived—indeed, at its simplest it is essentially a melody harmonized by the lower voices. Furthermore, the partsong is normally intended for performance with chorus rather than solo voices.

Another type of composition generally intended, like the madrigal, for solo voices was the Glee, a uniquely English creation which flourished in the eighteenth century as the convivial music of all-male musical societies. *Music all powerful* is a typical example of this form, with its several sections clearly defined by full cadences and a change of time signature. Although a composer such as John Goss was writing glees well into the nineteenth century, the partsong (or choral song, as it was often called) quickly established itself as more suitable for mixed-voice music-making, which was now on the increase. Composers generally wrote in several idioms and few were like William Horsley or Samuel Webbe (the latter not represented here) who were known almost exclusively as glee composers. Henry Bishop produced a vast amount of music for the stage from which much was extracted and published variously as songs, glees, and partsongs. John Hatton toured extensively as a pianist and *buffo* vocalist (including a solo tour of the USA) and composed many songs (*To Anthea, Simon the Cellarer*) and partsongs; these reveal a clear melodic gift, though his remains a minor talent at best.

More distinguished musical minds began treating the choral song as something of musical substance. A sensibility for choral texture begins to colour the partsongs of Macfarren, Benedict and Sterndale Bennett, who, taking what they would from madrigal and glee, created idiomatic compositions in a genuinely new 'Victorian' style. At the same time, the influence of Mendelssohn on English music began to be felt, an influence that was strong, long-lasting, and not universally approved of. His presence was most pronounced in the world of oratorio and instrumental composition, but his partsongs, supplied with English translations, became immensely popular (as did their originals in Germany). Mendelssohn was also acquainted with the English glee tradition and counted William Horsley among his musical friends. The German equivalent of the Glee Club, the *Liedertafel*, was founded by Mendelssohn's teacher, Karl Friedrich Zelter. But Mendelssohn himself was attempting something altogether larger, and in his partsongs headed *'Im Freien zu singen'* was keen to break free from the chamber music associations evoked by the use of voices with piano (the norm for Schubert's compositions for mixed voices).

William Sterndale Bennett is still an unduly neglected figure in the history of English music. He was a lifelong friend of Mendelssohn, who held him in high esteem, as did Schumann. Amongst his works is the sacred cantata *The Woman of Samaria*, with its well-known quartet 'God is a spirit', some very fine piano music (including four concertos), and a number of attractive songs. The influence of Mendelssohn is undeniable, though hardly a reason for ignoring one of the few nineteenth-century English composers who was widely admired abroad. Bennett's influence on English musical life has also not been fully appreciated—he produced the first English language edition of the *St Matthew Passion*, was director of the (now Royal) Philharmonic Society, founded the Bach Society (now the Bach Choir), and was Principal of the Royal Academy of Music.

The exchange of music and musicians between England and Germany was a strong feature of the nineteenth century—England being regarded primarily as an important market for performers, while Germany perhaps enjoying the greater prestige for its composers. But Hugo Pierson, potentially one of England's most significant *lied* composers, emigrated to Germany, so the exchange was in both directions. Julius Benedict moved the opposite way. He was born in Stuttgart and studied under Weber, later publishing a study of his mentor. He eventually settled in England, became a British subject, and was even knighted in 1871. His most famous work was the opera *The Lily of Killarney*, produced in London in 1862, from which we still hear the popular duet 'The moon has raised her lamp above'.

Although he is hardly known today, George Macfarren was one of the mid-century's leading figures, producing comic operas (*Robin Hood, She stoops to conquer*), oratorios (*St John the Baptist* is the finest of these), symphonies, and chamber music. His series of Shakespeare settings, two of which are included here, shows an adventurous sense of texture and a spirited, fresh response to words. His younger brother, Walter, was also a noted composer.

In partsongs such as *Sweet and low* and *The long day closes* we find the epitome of what is understood by the term 'Victorian partsong'. Opinion seems divided as to their true musical worth, but of their genre they are both typical and perfect examples. Tennyson's cradle song could not be imagined in a more sympathetic setting, while Sullivan's music so far transcends the banality of Chorley's poem as to create a minor masterpiece. Many of Sullivan's Savoy operas contain partsongs or madrigals, but he composed a handful of separate pieces, two of which join *The long day closes* here as examples of his melodious art, brushed at auspicious moments by the delectable spirit of late-Victorian harmony.

In the music of Parry and Stanford we veer rapidly towards the Edwardian era and the enduring sense that 'ripeness is all'. Parry was a prolific composer—had he composed less, he might be more widely performed today. However, his reputation is sustained by such works as *Blest pair of sirens, Jerusalem,* some of the solo songs, and the *Songs of Farewell* (which might easily have been represented here, were there not other purely secular pieces with an equal claim). His style carries more than a trace of Brahms, filtered through the atmosphere of an English country house (ungenerous perhaps, but not entirely untrue), but at its best this music has passion, distinction, and the courage of its convictions. He also showed a discriminating taste in his choice of poetry, which included the Elizabethans and (as here) some of the finest nineteenth-century writing.

Also of a Brahmsian cast, especially in his church music, Stanford's is a refreshing voice with a deft sense of harmonic inflection. The impressionist tinges of *The blue bird* show a loosening of harmonic vocabulary which was soon to be extended by his contemporary Elgar, and the younger generation in the persons of Vaughan Williams and Delius.

With Elgar himself we reach an acknowledged master, although his partsongs can hardly be described as well-known today. They are, however, magnificent for their scale and, pleasingly, the texts chosen are generally of a high standard (certainly when compared with his solo songs).

Three of Elgar's younger contemporaries conclude this collection. Charles Wood was a prolific composer of church music (much of it still in use in our cathedrals) in which he tastefully indulges a passion for Tudor polyphony. He also wrote a successful madrigal, *If love be dead,* and his song *Ethiopia saluting the colours* remains an active member of the standard English song repertoire. The Scottish composer Hamish MacCunn was a keen follower of Wagner, and his opera *Jeanie Deans* (produced in Edinburgh in 1894) is probably his finest achievement. He was also the composer of some powerful, if ultimately rather derivative, songs and is perhaps at his best when the Scots influence is at its strongest, tempering the Wagnerian steel. Samuel Coleridge-Taylor's enduring monument, institutionalized by Sir Malcolm Sargent, is the cantata *Hiawatha's Wedding Feast.* He was of mixed West African and English descent, a heritage he explored in his *Bamboula Rhapsody,* the *African Romances* (songs), and the *Twenty-four Negro Melodies* for piano. From amongst a handful of partsongs, the chords of *Summer is gone,* piled high with thirds like a tall building perched on a landslide, seem a fitting conclusion to an anthology of romantic partsongs and, indeed, to an era.

If any final word in favour of English romantic partsongs were needed beyond the observation that they are rewarding to sing and to listen to, we might remember that music is a social activity before it is an object of cultural homage and critical evaluation. Today's art music, with only a few exceptions, is about as far removed from the general public as it could ever expect to be (though the general public is not too worried about this, of course). Music-making, as distinct from concert-going, played a far higher part in nineteenth-century domestic life than it does today. We have cause to reflect on this, and consider that in this vital respect at least, the Victorians still have something important to give us.

Paul Hillier
Rodmell, Sussex

1. O sing unto my roundelay

MADRIGAL

THOMAS CHATTERTON

SAMUEL WESLEY

Moderately slow

SOPRANO 1
O sing___ un-to my roun-de - lay, my roun - de - lay,

SOPRANO 2
O sing___ un-to my roun-de - lay, my roun - de - lay,

ALTO
O sing, O sing un-to my roun-de - lay, O drop the

TENOR
O drop the

BASS

Printed in Great Britain
OXFORD UNIVERSITY PRESS, MUSIC DEPARTMENT, GREAT CLARENDON STREET, OXFORD OX2 6DP

9
Loud
- lay, Drop the briny tear with me, O sing unto my roun - de -
Loud
- lay, O drop the briny tear with me, O sing unto my roun - de -
Loud
- lay, O sing, O sing unto my
Loud
Drop the briny tear with me, with me, O
Loud
O sing unto my
13
- lay, unto my roun - de - lay;
Soft
- lay, unto my roun - de - lay; Drop the briny tear with me;
Soft
roun - de - lay, my roun - de - lay; Drop the briny tear with me;
sing unto my roun - de - lay;
Soft
roun - de - lay; Drop the briny tear with me;
17
Loud
Dance no more, dance no more on ho - li - day, dance no more on
Loud
Dance no more, dance no more on ho - li - day, dance no more on
Loud
Dance no more, dance no more on ho - li - day, dance no more on
Loud
Dance no more, dance no more on ho - li - day, dance no more on
Loud
Dance no more on ho - li - day, dance no more on

21
ho - li - day; Like a — run - ning ri - ver
ho - li - day; Like a run - ning ri - ver — be, — a — run - ning, run - ning ri - ver
ho - li - day;
ho - li - day; Like a run - ning, — run - ning ri - ver —
ho - li - day;
25
be, a run - ning ri - ver, like a run - ning — ri - ver be;
be, a — run - ning ri - ver, a run - ning — ri - ver be;
Like a run - ning ri - ver — be, like a running ri - ver be;
be, — like a run - ning ri - ver be;
Like a run - ning — ri - ver — be, a run - ning ri - ver be;
29
Soft
My love is dead, Gone — to — his death - bed, All un -
Soft
My love is dead, Gone — to — his death - bed, All un -
Soft
My love is dead, Gone — to his — death - bed,
Soft
My love is dead, All un -
[Soft]
Gone — to his death - bed.

34
- der the wil - low tree, all un - der the wil - low tree.
- der the wil - low tree, all un - der the wil - low tree.
Loud
Un - der the wil - low tree. Like a
8
- der the wil - low tree, un - der the wil - low tree.
Loud
Like a run - ning ri - ver
38
Loud
O sing un - to my roun - de -
Loud
Like a run - ning ri - ver be. O sing un - to my roun - de -
run - ning ri - ver be. O sing, O sing un - to my roun - de -
Loud
8
O sing, sing un - to my roun - de -
be, a run - ning ri - ver be. Sing un - to my roun - de -
42
- lay; Drop the bri - ny tear with me;
Soft
My love is dead, Gone
- lay; O drop the bri - ny tear with me;
Soft
My love is dead, Gone,
- lay;
Soft
My love is dead, Gone,
8
- lay; Drop the bri - ny tear with me;
- lay;

47
— to his death - bed, All un - der the wil - low_ tree, all un - der the wil - low
gone to his death - bed, All un - der the wil - low_ tree, all un - der the wil - low_
gone to his death - bed, All un - der the wil - low
Soft
All un - der the wil - low tree, all un - der the wil - low
Soft
All un - der the wil - low
52
Loud
Soft
tree, My love, — my love is dead, Gone to his death - bed, All un - der the wil-low
Loud
Soft
tree, My love, — my love is dead, Gone to his death - bed, All un-der the wil-low
Loud
Soft
tree, My love is dead, Gone to — his death - bed, Un - der the wil-low_
Loud
Soft
tree,_ My love is dead, Gone to his death - bed, Un-der the wil-low
Loud
tree, My love is dead, Gone to his death - bed,
58
tree, all un - der the wil - - low tree, My love is
tree, all un - der the wil - - low tree, My love is
tree, all un - der_ the_ wil - - low tree, My love is
Soft
tree, My love is dead,
[Soft]
Soft
All un - der the — wil - low tree, My love is dead,

63
dead, Gone to his death - bed, All un - der the wil - low tree, all
dead, Gone, gone to his death - bed, All un - der the wil - low tree, all
dead, Gone, gone to his death - bed,
All un - der the wil - low tree, all
68
Loud
un - der the wil - low tree, My love, my love is dead, Gone to his death -
un - der the wil - low tree, My love, my love is dead, Gone to his death -
My love is dead, Gone to his death -
un - der the wil - low tree, My love is dead, Gone to his death -
My love is dead, Gone to his death -
73
- bed, Un - der the wil - low, wil - low tree, un - der the wil - low, wil - low
- bed, Un - der the wil - low, wil - low tree, un - der the wil - low, wil - low
- bed, Un - der, un - der the wil - low, wil - low tree, un - der the wil - low,
- bed, All un - der the wil - low tree, all un - der the wil - low
- bed,

77
tree, un - der the wil - low, the wil - low tree, un - der the
tree, un - der the wil - low, the wil - low tree, un - der the
wil - low tree, the wil - low tree, all un - der,
tree, un - der the wil - low tree, un
All un - der the wil - low tree,
81
Loud
wil - low, wil - low tree, un - der the wil - low, wil - low tree, un - der the
wil - low, wil - low tree, un - der the
un - der the wil - low tree, the wil - low tree, un -
- der the wil - low tree, all un - der the wil - low tree, un -
85
wil - low tree, the wil - low tree.
will - low tree, the wil - low tree.
- der the wil - low tree, the wil - low tree.
- der the wil - low tree, all un - der the wil - low tree.
all un - der the wil - low tree.

2. Slow fresh fount

GLEE

BEN JONSON

WILLIAM HORSLEY

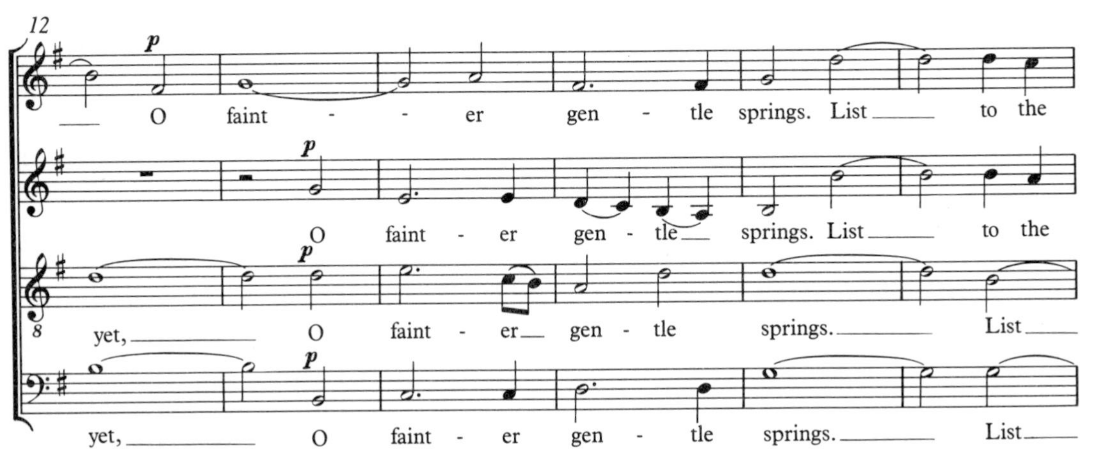

18
hea - vy part, list to the hea - vy part the mu - sic
hea - vy part, list to the hea - vy part the mu - sic
to the hea - vy part, list to the hea - vy part the mu - sic
to the hea - vy part, list to the hea - vy part the mu - sic
24
pp
bears; Woe weeps out, woe weeps out, weeps out her de -
bears; Woe weeps out, weeps, weeps out
bears; Woe weeps, woe weeps out her de -
bears; Woe weeps out, woe weeps out her de - ci - sion
30
- ci - sion when she sings. Droop herbs and flowers,
her de - ci - sion when she sings. Droop herbs and flowers,
- ci - sion when she sings. Droop herbs and flowers,
when she sings. Droop herbs and flowers,

35
Fall grief in showers, Our beau - ty is not ours.
Fall grief in showers, Our beau - ty is not ours.
Fall grief in showers, Our beau - ty is not ours.
Fall grief in showers, Our beau - ty is not ours.
41
p
O could I still like melt - ing
O could I still like melt - - ing
O could I still like melt - ing
O could I still like melt - ing
46
pp
p
snow up - on some crag - gy hill Fall down, fall
snow up - on some crag - gy hill Fall down, fall
snow up - on some crag - gy hill Fall down, fall
snow up - on some crag - gy hill Fall down, fall

51
down,
since sum - mer's pride is now a with - ered
down, since sum - mer's pride is now a with - ered, with - ered
down,
down,
since sum - mer's
55
daff - o - dil,
since sum - mer's pride is now a
daff - o - dil,
since sum - mer's pride is now, is now a with - ered
since sum - mer's pride is now, is now a with - ered daff - o - dil,
pride is now a with - ered daff - o - dil,
since sum - mer's
59
with - ered, with - ered daff - o - dil,
daff - o - dil,
since sum - mer's pride is now a with - ered
since sum - mer's pride is now, is now a with - ered daff - o - dil,
pride's a with - ered daff - o - dil,
since sum - mer's pride is now a

63
since sum - mer's pride is now a with - - - - - -
daff - o - dil, a with - ered daff - o - dil, since sum - mer's
a with - ered daff - o - dil, since sum - mer's pride's a with - ered
with - ered, with - ered daff - o - dil, a with - ered
67
- ered,
with - - - - - -
pride is now a with - ered, with-ered daff - o - dil, since sum - mer's
daff - o - dil, since sum - mer's pride's a with - ered daff - o - dil,
daff - o - dil, since sum - mer's pride is now a with - ered,
71
- ered,
now a with - ered daff - o - dil.
pride is now, is now a with - ered, with - - ered daff - o - dil.
since sum- mer's pride is now a with - ered, with - ered daff - o - dil.
with - - - - - - - ered daff - o - dil.

3. Music, all powerful

GLEE

H. K. WHITE

THOMAS F. WALMISLEY

dim.
ff
fur - ious rage dis - arm, fierce an - - - - ger's
fur - ious rage dis - arm, fierce an - ger's fur - ious
[dim.]
an - ger's rage dis - arm, fierce an - ger's fur - ious
fur - ious rage dis - arm, dis - arm, fierce an - ger's fur - ious rage, fierce
Più moto
p
f
rage dis - arm.
rage dis - arm. At her com - mand, the
[f]
rage dis - arm. At her com -
an - ger's rage dis - arm. At her com - mand, the
She stirs to bat - tle, or she lulls to
var - ious pas - sions lie, She stirs to bat - tle, or lulls to
- mand, the pas - sions lie, She stirs to bat - tle,
var - ious pas - sions lie, She stirs to bat - tle,

28
p
p dolce
peace, or she lulls to peace, or
f
p
f
peace, she stirs to bat-tle, or lulls to peace, she stirs to bat-tle,
f
f
she stirs to bat-tle, she stirs to bat-tle,
f
f
she stirs to bat-tle, she stirs to bat-tle,
32
3
she lulls, she lulls to peace, Melts the charm'd
p
or she lulls to peace, Melts the charm'd
or she lulls to peace,
or she lulls to peace, the
37
cresc.
f
soul to thrill - ing ec - sta-sy, And bids the jar-ring world's harsh
[cresc.]
f
soul to thrill - ing ec - sta-sy, And bids the jar-ring world's harsh
[cresc.]
f
to thrill - ing ec - sta-sy, And bids the jar-ring world's harsh
f
f
soul to thrill - - ing ec - sta-sy, And bids the jar-ring world's harsh

42
dim.
cresc.
clang - our cease, Melts the charm'd soul to thrill - ing
clang - our cease, Melts the charm'd soul to thrill - ing
clang - our cease, Melts the charm'd soul to thrill - ing
clang - our cease, to thrill - ing
47
ec - sta - sy, And bids the jar - ring world's harsh clang - our cease,
ec - sta - sy, And bids the jar - ring world's harsh clang - our cease,
ec - sta - sy, And bids the jar - ring world's harsh clang - our cease.
ec - sta - sy, And bids the jar - ring world's harsh clang - our cease,
52
rit.
Tempo primo, con espressione
p dolce
cease, cease. Then
cease, cease. Soft thro' the dell the dy - ing strains re - tire, Then
Soft thro' the dell the dy - ing strains re - tire, Then
cease. Then

58
burst ma - jes - tic, in the va - ried swell,
p
burst ma - jes - tic, in the va - ried swell, Now,
burst ma - jes - tic, in the va - ried swell,
burst ma - jes - tic, in the va - ried swell,
62
p
Now, breathe me - lo - dious as the Gre - cian lyre,
breathe me - lo - dious as the Gre - cian lyre,
[p]
Or
66
rit.
p
dim.
Or on the ear, in sink - ing ca - dence dwell.
[p]
dim.
Or on the ear, in sink - ing ca - dence dwell.
dim.
on the ear, in sink - ing ca - dence dwell.

70
Andante cantabile
[p]
Oh! sure - ly Har - mo - ny from Heav'n was sent, To
[p]
Oh! sure - ly Har - mo - ny from Heav'n was sent, To
[p]
Oh! sure - ly Har - mo - ny from Heav'n was sent, To
[p]
Oh! sure - ly Har - mo - ny from Heav'n was sent, To
74
cheer the soul when tir'd with hu - man strife;
cheer the soul when tir'd with hu - man strife;
cheer the soul when tir'd with hu - man strife; Oh!
cheer the soul when tir'd with hu - man strife;
78
Oh! sure - ly Har - mo - ny from Heav'n was sent, To
Oh! sure - ly Har - mo - ny from Heav'n was sent, To
sure - ly Har - mo - ny from Heav'n was sent, To
Oh! sure - ly Har - mo - ny from Heav'n was sent, To

82
cheer the soul when tir'd with hu - man strife; To
cheer the soul when tir'd with hu - man strife;
cheer the soul when tir'd with hu - man strife;
cheer the soul when tir'd with hu - man strife; To
86
cresc.
soothe the way - ward heart by sor - row rent, And
the way - ward heart by sor - row rent, And
the way - ward heart by sor - row rent, And
cresc.
soothe the way - ward heart by sor - row rent, And
90
soft - en down, and soft - en down the rug - ged
soft - en down, and soft - en down the rug - ged
soft - en down the rug - ged
soft - en down the rug - ged

95
pp
road of life, soft - en, soft - en, soft - en
pp
road of life, soft - en, soft - en, soft - en
pp
8
road of life, soft - en, soft - en, soft - en
p
road of life, soft - - en down, soft - - en
100
cresc. sf p
down the rug - ged road, and soft - - - en,
cresc. sf p
down the rug - ged road, and soft - - - en,
cresc. sf p
8
down the rug - ged road, and soft - - - en,
cresc. sf p
down the rug - ged road, soft - - - en, and
105
rit.
soft - en down the rug - ged road of life.
soft - en down the rug - ged road of life.
8
soft - en down the rug - ged road of life.
soft - en down the rug - ged road of life.

4. Home, sweet home

JOHN HOWARD PAYNE

HENRY BISHOP
Harmonized by T. CRAMPTON

15
f
p
f
met with else - where. Home, home, sweet, sweet home; There's no place like
met with else - where. Home, home, sweet, sweet home; There's no place like
met with else - where. Home, home, sweet, sweet home; There's no place like
met with else - where. Home, home, sweet, sweet home; There's no place like
21
mf
home, There's no place like home. An ex - ile from home, splen - dour
home, There's no place like home. An ex - ile from home, splen - dour
home, There's no place like home. An ex - ile from home, splen - dour
home, There's no place like home. An ex - ile from home, splen - dour
26
daz - zles in vain; O give me my lone - ly thatch'd cot - tage a -
daz - zles in vain; thatch'd cot - tage a -
daz - zles in vain; O give me my lone - ly thatch'd cot - tage a -
daz - zles in vain; O give me my lone - ly thatch'd cot - tage a -

31
-gain. The birds sing-ing gai-ly, come_ at my call, And
-gain. The birds sing-ing gai-ly, come_ at my call, And
-gain. And
-gain. The birds sing-ing gai-ly, come at my call, And
36
give me the peace of mind, dear-er than all. Home, home,_
give me_ the peace of mind, dear-er than all. Home, home,_
give me_ the_ peace of mind,_ dear-er than all. Home,_ home,_
give me the peace of mind, dear-er than all. Home,_ home,
41
sweet, sweet home; There's no place like home,_ There's no_ place like home.
sweet, sweet home; There's no place like home,_ There's no place like home.
sweet, sweet home; There's no place like home,_ There's no place like home.
sweet, sweet home; There's no place like home,_ There's no place like home.

5. Who shall have my lady fair

ANON. ROBERT PEARSALL

8
p
cresc.
la - dy fair, When the leaves are green, when the leaves are green?
la - dy fair, When the leaves are green, when the leaves are green.
p
cresc.
I should win my la - dy fair, When the leaves are green?
I; I won't bu-ry my la - dy fair, When the leaves are green.
p
cresc.
la - dy fair, When the leaves, the leaves are green, when the leaves are
la - dy fair, When the leaves, the leaves are green, when the leaves are
p
cresc.
I should win my la - dy fair, When the leaves are green, when the leaves are
I; I won't bu-ry my la - dy fair, When the leaves are green, when the leaves are
13
f
Who shall win my la - dy, when the leaves are green?
Will you bu - ry my la - dy, when the leaves are green?
f
p
Who shall win my la - dy, when the leaves are green? Say
Will you bu-ry my la - dy, when the leaves are green? Say
f
p
green? Who shall win my la - dy, when the leaves are green? Say
green. Will you bu-ry my la - dy, when the leaves are green? Say
f
green? Who shall win my la - dy, when the leaves are green?
green. Will you bu - ry my la - dy, when the leaves are green?
17
p
cresc.
f
Not you, not you, not you, no, no, The brav - est man that
will you, will you, will you? Why so? I'd ra - ther mar-ry my
cresc.
f
who, say who, say who? Why so? The brav - est man that
who, say who, say who? No, no! I'd ra - ther mar-ry my
cresc.
f
who, say who, say who? Why so? The brav - est man that
who, say who, say who? No, no! I'd ra - ther mar- ry my
cresc.
f
Say who? Why so? The brav - est man that
Say who? No, no! I'd ra - ther mar-ry my

22
dim.
best love can Shall win my la - - dy fair.
la - dy fair, E'en though the trees were bare.
dim.
best love can Shall win my la - - - - dy fair.
la - dy fair, E'en though the trees were bare.
dim.
best love can Shall win, shall win my la - dy fair.
la - dy fair, E'en though, e'en though the trees were bare.
dim.
best love can Shall win, shall win, shall win my la - dy fair.
la - dy fair, E'en though, e'en though, e'en though the trees were bare.
28
p
fz
Dan - dir - ly, dan - dir - ly, dan - dir - ly dan,
He shall mar - ry her,
She shall mar - ry a
p
fz
Dan - - - - - - dir - ly dan,
He shall mar - ry her,
She shall mar - ry a
p
fz
Dan - dir - ly, dan - dir - ly, dan - dir - ly dan,
He shall mar - ry her,
She shall mar - ry a
p
fz
Dan - dir - ly, dan - dir - ly, dan - dir - ly dan,
He shall mar - ry her,
She shall mar - ry a
31
f
he's the man;
pro - per man;
Dan - dir - ly, dan - dir - ly, dan - dir - ly dan,
f
he's the man;
pro - per man;
Dan - dir - ly, dan - dir - ly, dan - dir - ly dan,
f
he's the man;
pro - per man;
Dan - dir - ly, dan - dir - ly, dan - dir - ly dan,
f
he's the man;
pro - per man;
Dan - dir - ly, dan - dir - ly, dan - dir - ly dan,
he's the
pro - per

34
p
cresc.
When the leaves are green,
when the leaves are green,
When the leaves are green,
when the leaves are green,
When the leaves, the leaves are green,
when the leaves are
man,
man,
When the leaves are green,
38
f
He shall mar - ry my la - dy, when the leaves are green.
He shall mar - ry my la - dy, when the leaves are green.
green, He shall mar - ry my la - dy, when the leaves are green.
green, He shall mar - ry my la - dy, when the leaves are green.
42

6. Lay a garland

MADRIGAL

Words from Beaumont and Fletcher

ROBERT PEARSALL

12
Maid - ens, wil - low bran - - ches,
Maid - ens, wil - low bran - -
Maid - ens, wil - low
Maid - ens, wil - low
- ens, wil - low bran - ches wear,
Maid - ens, wil - low bran - ches wear, maid -
yew;
- - - - - mal yew;
17
wil - - - - - low bran - - -
- - ches wear; Say she
bran - - - - ches wear;
cresc.
bran - - - - ches wear; Say,
cresc.
maid - ens, wil - low bran - -
- ens, wil - low bran - - - - - - ches wear;
Maid - - ens, wil - low bran - - - - - -
cresc.
Maid - ens, wil - low bran - -

22
dim.
- - ches wear; Say, say she di - - - ed true,
cresc.
dim.
di - - ed true, say she di - - - ed true,
dim.
Say she di - ed true,
say she di - ed true, Her
dim.
- - ches wear; Say she di - ed true,
cresc.
[dim.]
Say she di - ed true, say she di - ed true,
[dim.]
- - ches wear; Say she di - - - ed true,
dim.
- ches wear; Say she di - ed true,
28
cresc.
Her love
cresc.
Her love
[cresc.]
Her love was false,
cresc.
love
[p]
cresc.
Her love was
cresc.
Her love
Her love
Her love was

35
was false, but she was firm.
was false, but she was firm.
her love was false, but she was firm. Up-
dim.
was false, but she was
false, her love was false, but she was firm.
dim.
was false, but she was
dim.
was false, but she was
false, but she was
42
Up - on her bu ried
Up-on her bu - ried bo -
[cresc.]
- on her bu - ried bo - dy lie,
firm. Up - on her bu - ried
[cresc.]
Up-on her bu - ried bo - dy lie,
firm. Up - on her bo - dy lie,
cresc.
firm. Up - on her bu - ried
cresc.
firm. Up - on her bu - ried bo -
cresc.
p
[p]

48
bo - dy lie light - ly, thou gen - - tle
- dy lie light - ly, thou gen - tle
cresc.
lie light - ly, thou gen - - tle
bo - dy lie light - ly, thou gen - - - tle
cresc.
lie light - ly, thou gen - - - - - tle, gen - tle
thou gen - - - - - tle
bo - - - dy lie, thou gen - - - - tle
- - dy lie light - ly, thou gen - - - - tle
53
p
earth, thou gen - - - - - - - - tle earth.
p
earth, thou gen - - - - - - - tle earth.
p
earth, thou gen - - - - tle, gen - tle earth.
p
earth, thou gen - - - - tle, gen - tle earth.
p
earth, thou gen - tle earth.
p
earth, thou gen - - - tle earth, thou gen - - tle earth.
p
earth, thou gen - tle, gen - - - - tle earth.
p
earth, thou gen - tle, gen - - - tle earth.

7. Sir Patrick Spens

BALLAD-DIALOGUE

Traditional Scottish Ballad

ROBERT PEARSALL

7 CHORUS 1
sail this new ship of mine?'
sail this ship of mine?'
cap - tain bold To sail this ship of mine?'
To sail this ship of mine?'
sail this new ship of mine?'
CHORUS 2
mf
Then up and spake an eld - ern knight,
mf
Then up and spake an eld - ern knight,
mf
Then up and spake an eld - ern knight, Sat
mf
Then up and spake an eld - ern knight,
mf
Then up and spake an eld - ern knight,
10 CHORUS 2
cresc.
Sat at the King's right knee: 'Sir Pat - rick Spens is the
cresc.
Sat at the King's right knee: 'Sir
cresc.
at the King's right knee: 'Sir Pat - rick Spens is the best, is the
cresc.
'Sir Pat - rick Spens is the best, is the
cresc.
Sat at the King's right knee: 'Sir Pat - rick is the

13 (CHORUS 2)
best sail - or That ev - er, that ev - er sail'd the sea, that
Pat - rick is the best That ev - er sail'd the sea, the best That ev - er sail'd, that
best sail - or That ev - - - - er sail'd the sea, that
best That ev - er sail'd the sea, that ev - er sail'd the sea, that
best sail - or That ev - er, ev - er sail'd the sea, that ev - er,
16 CHORUS 1
f
The King has writ-ten a broad let - ter, And seal'd it with
The King has writ-ten a broad let - ter, And seal'd it
The King has writ-ten a broad let - ter, And seal'd it
The King has writ-ten a broad let - ter, And seal'd it
The King has writ-ten a broad let - ter, And seal'd it
CHORUS 2
ev - er sail'd the sea!' The King has writ-ten a broad let - ter, And seal'd it
ev - er sail'd the sea!' The King has writ-ten a broad let - ter, And seal'd it
ev - er sail'd the sea!' The King has writ-ten a broad let - ter, And seal'd it with
ev - er sail'd the sea!' The King has writ - ten a broad let - ter, And seal'd it
ev - er sail'd the sea!' The King has writ - ten a broad let - ter, And seal'd it

20
CHORUS 1
p
___ his hand, And sent it to Sir Pat - rick Spens, Who was
p
with his hand, And sent it to Sir Pat - rick, Who was walk - ing,
p
with his hand, Who was
p
with his hand, Who was
p
with his hand, Who was
CHORUS 2
p
with his hand, And sent ___ it to Sir Pat - - rick, Who was
p
with his hand, And sent it to Sir Pat - rick, Who was walk - ing,
p
___ his hand, Who was
p
with his hand, Who was
p
with his hand, Who was

23
walk - ing on the strand. 'To Nor- a - way, to Nor - - - - - - a - way, to
walk - ing on the strand.
walk - ing on the strand.
walk - ing on the strand.
walk - ing on the strand.
walk - ing on the strand. 'To Nor - a - way, to Nor - a - way, to
walk - ing on the strand. 'To Nor - a - way, to Nor - a - way, to
walk - ing on the strand. 'To Nor - a - way, to
walk - ing on the strand. 'To Nor - a - way, to Nor - a - way, to
walk - ing on the strand. 'To Nor - a-way, to Nor - a - way, to

27
CHORUS 1
Nor - a - way, o'er the foam.
CHORUS 2
Nor - a - way, o'er the foam, The Prin - cess fair of
Nor - a - way, o'er the foam, The Prin-cess fair of Nor - a - way, 'Tis thou, thou
8 Nor - a - way, o'er the foam, The Prin - cess of
8 Nor - a - way, o'er the foam, The Prin - cess, the Prin-cess fair of
Nor - a - way, o'er the foam, The Prin - cess fair of

30
CHORUS 1
f
'O! who is it has done this deed, And
'O! who is it has done this deed, And
'O! who is it has done this deed, And
'O! who is it has done this deed,
'O! who is it has done this deed, And
CHORUS 2
Nor - a-way,'Tis thou,'tis thou must bring her home.'
must bring her home, 'tis thou must bring her home.'
Nor - a - way, 'Tis thou, 'tis thou must bring her home.'
Nor - a-way,'Tis thou, 'tis thou must bring her home.'
Nor - a - way, 'Tis thou,'tis thou must bring her home.'
34 CHORUS 1
told the King of me? To send us out at this time of the
told the King of me? To send us out, to send us
told the King of me? To send us out, to send us out at this time of the
To send us out at this time of the year, to send us out, To
told the King of me? To send us out at this time of the

38 (CHORUS 1)
year, To sail up - on the sea, to sail up - on the
out this time of year, To sail, this time of year, To sail up - on the
year, to send us out To sail up - on the
sail up - on the sea, send us out To sail up - on the
year, to send, to send us out this time of year up - on the
41 CHORUS 1
sea!'
sea!'
sea!'
sea!'
sea!'
CHORUS 2
p
They had not sail'd a league, a league, A league but bare - ly three, When the
They had not sail'd a league, a league, A league but bare - ly three, When the
They had not sail'd a league, a league, A league but bare - ly three, When the
They had not sail'd a league, a league, A league but bare-ly three, When the
They had not sail'd a league, a league, A league but bare - ly three, When the

45
CHORUS 1
ff
The anchors brake,
The anchors brake,
The anchors brake,
The anchors brake,
The anchors brake,
CHORUS 2
cresc.
sky grew dark, and the wind blew loud, And gur - ly* grew the sea. The anchors
sky grew dark, and the wind blew loud, And gur - ly grew the sea. The anchors
sky grew dark, and the wind blew loud, And gur - ly grew the sea. The anchors
sky grew dark, and the wind blew loud, And gur - ly grew the sea. The anchors
sky grew dark, and the wind blew loud, And gur - ly grew the sea. The anchors
f

* stormy

49 CHORUS 1
the top-masts lap, 'Twas such a dead - ly storm.
thetop-mastslap, 'Twas such a dead - ly, dead - ly storm.
thetop-mastslap, 'Twas such a dead - ly, dead - ly storm.
thetop-mastslap, 'Twas such a dead - ly, dead - ly_ storm.
the top-masts lap, 'Twas such a dead - ly, dead - ly_ storm.
CHORUS 2
brake,_ the top-masts lap,_ 'Twas such a dead - ly storm.
brake, the top-masts lap, 'Twas such a dead - ly storm.
brake, the top-masts lap, 'Twas such a dead - ly storm. And the
brake, the top-masts lap, 'Twas such a dead - ly storm. And the waves came
brake,_ the top-masts lap,_ 'Twas such a dead - lystorm. And the waves came o'er_ the_
53 CHORUS 2
And the waves came o'er the bro - - - ken ship, Till all her sides were
And the waves, the waves came_ o'er the bro - ken ship, Till_ her sides were
waves came o'er,_ came o'er the bro - ken ship, Till all her sides were
o'er_ the bro - ken_ ship,_ Till all her sides were torn, till all_ her sides were
bro - ken ship, Till all her sides were torn, The waves came o'er the ship, Till all her sides were

57
CHORUS 1
The la-dies wrang their fin - - gers white, The maid - ens tore their
The la-dies wrang their fin - - gers white, The maid - ens tore their
The la-dies wrang their fin - gers white, The maid-ens tore their
The la-dies wrang their fin - gers white, The maid - ens tore their
CHORUS 2
torn.
torn.
torn.
torn.
torn.

61
CHORUS 1
p
All for the sake of their true loves, For them they'll see no more.
f
O!
hair,
f
O!
hair,
All for their true loves, For them they'll see no more.
f
O!
8
hair,
f
O! for - ty
8
hair,
f
O!
CHORUS 2
p
All for the sake of their true loves, For them they'll see no more.
f
O!
p
All for the sake of their true loves, For them they'll see no more.
f
O!
f
O!
8
f
O!
8
p
For them they'll see no more.
f
O!

65
for - ty miles from A - ber - deen 'Tis fif - ty fa - thom deep.
for - ty miles from A - ber - deen 'Tis fif - ty fa - thom deep.
for - ty miles from A - ber - deen 'Tis fif - ty fa - thom deep.
miles from A - ber - deen 'Tis fif - ty fa - thom deep.
for - ty miles from A - ber - deen 'Tis fif - ty fa - thom deep.
for - ty miles from A - ber - deen 'Tis fif - ty fa - thom deep, And
for - ty miles from A - ber - deen 'Tis fif - ty fa - thom deep, And
for - ty miles from A - ber - deen 'Tis fif - ty fa - thom deep, And
for - ty miles from A - ber - deen 'Tis fif - ty fa - thom deep, And
for - ty miles from A - ber - deen 'Tis fif - ty fa - thom deep, And

69
CHORUS 1
Risoluto (𝅗𝅥 =80)
p
With his
p
With his com -
CHORUS 2
Risoluto (𝅗𝅥 =80)
there lies brave Sir Pat - rick Spens, With his com -
p
there lies brave Sir Pat - rick, With
p
there lies brave Sir Pat - rick Spens, With his com - rades
p
there lies brave Sir Pat - rick Spens, With his com - rades
p
there lies brave Sir Pat - rick Spens, With his com -

74
pp
p
[p]
com - rades at his feet.
With his com - rades at his feet.
With his com - rades at his feet.
- - - rades, his com - - - rades at his feet.
at his feet.
- rades at his feet.
his com - - - rades at his feet.
at his feet, with his com - rades at his feet.
at his feet.
- - - rades at his feet.

8. List! for the breeze

GLEE

Words from the Spanish

JOHN GOSS

13
cresc.
sails, thro' the light fo - liage sails, thro' the
sails, the fo - liage sails, thro' the
thro' the light fo - liage, the fo - liage sails, thro' the
thro' the light fo - liage sails, thro' the
p
17
1
2
mf
fo - liage sails; sails; Hid - den a -
fo - liage sails; sails; Hid - den a -
fo - liage sails; sails; Hid - den a -
fo - liage sails; sails; Hid - den a -
20
[p] dolce
-midst the for - est green War - ble,
-midst the for - est green War - ble,
-midst the for - est green War - ble,
-midst the for - est green War -
p

24
pp
war - ble the night - in - gales,
war - ble the
pp
war - ble the night - in - gales,
war - -
8
pp
war - ble the night - - - in - gales,
war - -
dolce
pp
- - - ble the night - in - gales, war - ble, war - -
28
f
night - in-gales,
war - ble the night - in-gales,
Hid - den a -
f
- - - ble, war - ble the night - - in - gales, Hid - den a -
f
- - - ble, war - ble the night - - in - gales, Hid - den a -
f
- - - ble, war - ble the night - - in - gales, Hid - den a -
32
dim.
p
- midst the for - est green War - ble,
dim.
p
- midst the for - est green War - -
dim.
p
- midst, a - midst the for - est green War - ble,
dim.
p
- midst the for - est green, the for - est green

36
cresc.
war - - - - - - ble the night - in - gales, war - ble,
- - - - - - - - ble the night - in - gales, war - -
war - - - - - - ble the night - in - gales, war - ble,
War - - - - - - ble the night - in - gales,
40
war - - - - - - - - - ble the night - in - gales,
- - - - - - - - - ble the night - in - gales, war - ble the
war - - - - - - - - - ble the night - in - gales,
[cresc.]
war - - - - - - - - - ble the night - in - gales,
44
Slower
p
f
war - ble - the night - in-gales, war-ble the night - in - gales.
night - in - gales, the night - in - gales.
the night - in - gales, the night - in - gales.
the night - in - gales, the night - in - gales.

9. Dirge for the faithful lover

BEAUMONT & FLETCHER

JULIUS BENEDICT

12
cresc.
you whose loves are dead, Weep and wring Ev' - ry hand,
[cresc.]
f
dead, And whiles I sing, Weep and wring, Ev' -
p
[cresc.]
f
dead, And whiles I sing, Weep and wring Ev' - ry hand, and
And whiles I sing, Weep and [cresc.] wring Ev'ry hand, and
p
[f]
dead, And whiles I sing, Weep and wring Ev' - ry hand, and
16
f
p
cresc.
ev' - ry head Bind with cy - press and sad yew, Rib - bons black and
p
[cresc.]
- ry head Bind with cy - press, with cy - press
p
[cresc.]
ev' - ry head Bind with cy - press, with cy - press
ev' ry head
p unis.
[cresc.]
ev' - ry head Bind with cy - press, with cy - press
20
f
dim.
pp
can - dles blue, For him that was of men most true.
f
dim.
pp
and sad yew, For him that was of men most true.
f
dim.
pp
and sad yew, For him that was of men most true.
f
dim.
pp
and sad yew, For him that was of men most true.

25
Come with hea - vy moan - ing, come with hea - vy moan - ing, And
cresc.
29
on his grave Let him have Sa - cri - fice of sighs and
f
34
groan - ing, of sighs and groan - ing.
dolce
Let him have fair

38
cresc.
flow'rs e - now, White and pur - ple, green and yel - low, For him that
cresc.
have fair flow'rs e - now, For him that
[cresc.]
flow'rs e - now, White and pur - ple, green and yel - low, For him that
[cresc.]
have fair flow'rs e - now, For him that
42
f dim. p
was of men most true, for him that was of
f dim. p
was of men most true, for him that was of
f dim. p
was of men most true, for him that was of
f dim. p
was of men most true, for him that was of
47
pp rall. assai Lento
men most true, of men, of men most true.
pp
men most true, of men, of men most true.
pp
men most true, of men, of men most true.
pp
men most true, of men, of men most true.

10. Stars of the summer night

HENRY LONGFELLOW

JOHN HATTON

15
dolce
sleeps! Stars of the sum - mer night!
pp
sleeps, my la - dy sleeps! She sleeps, my
pp
sleeps, my la - dy sleeps! She sleeps, my
pp
sleeps, my la - dy sleeps! She sleeps, my
20
pp
Hide, hide your gold - en light! She
la - dy sleeps, she sleeps, She
la - dy sleeps, she sleeps, She
la - dy sleeps, she sleeps, She
25
sleeps, my la - dy sleeps!
sleeps, my la - dy sleeps!
sleeps, my la - dy sleeps!
sleeps, my la - dy sleeps!

2. Moon of the summer night!
Far down yon western steeps,
Sink, sink in silver light!
She sleeps, my lady sleeps!

3. Wind of the summer night!
Where yonder woodbine creeps,
Fold, fold thy pinions light!
She sleeps, my lady sleeps!

4. Dreams of the summer night!
Tell her, her lover keeps watch!
While in slumbers light!
She sleeps, my lady sleeps!

11. An old romance

(Drei Volkslieder)

English text by
?Sabilla Novello

FELIX MENDELSSOHN
Op. 41 Nos. 2–4

PART I: O fly with me/*Entflieh' mit mir*

8
f
p
all to thee, And when a - far a - way we rove, O let my
Va - ter-haus, In wei - ter Fer - ne sei mein Herz Dir Va - - ter -
all to thee, And when a - far a - way we rove, O let my
Va - ter- haus, In wei - ter Fer - ne sei mein Herz Dir Va - ter -
all to thee, And when a - far a - way we rove, O let my
Va - ter- haus, In wei - ter Fer - ne sei mein Herz Dir Va - ter -
all to thee, And when a - far a - way we rove, O let my
Va - ter- haus, In wei - ter Fer - ne sei mein Herz Dir Va - ter -
12
heart be all to thee. But if thou wilt not,
- land und Va - ter - haus. Und fliehst du nicht, so
heart be all to thee. But if thou wilt not,
- land und Va - ter - haus. Und fliehst du nicht, so
heart be all to thee. But if thou wilt not,
- land und Va - ter - haus. Und fliehst du nicht, so
heart be all to thee. But if thou wilt not,
- land und Va - ter - haus. Und fliehst du nicht, so
16
here I'll die, And drea - ry wilt thou be, and lone,
sterb' ich hier Und du bist ein - sam und al - lein;
here I'll die, And drea - ry wilt thou be, and lone,
sterb' ich hier Und du bist ein - sam und al - lein;
here I'll die, And drea - ry wilt thou be, and lone,
sterb' ich hier Und du bist ein - sam und al - lein;
here I'll die, And drea - ry wilt thou be, and lone,
sterb' ich hier Und du bist ein - sam und al - lein;

19
For tho' from home thou dost not fly, Home-joys are fled, when
Und bleibst du auch im Va - ter - haus, Wirst doch wie in der
For tho' from home thou dost not fly, Home-joys are fled, when
Und bleibst du auch im Va - ter - haus, Wirst doch wie in der
For tho' from home thou dost not fly, Home-joys are fled, when
Und bleibst du auch im Va - ter - haus, Wirst doch wie in der
For tho' from home thou dost not fly, Home-joys are fled, when
Und bleibst du auch im Va - ter - haus, Wirst doch wie in der
22
I am gone, For tho' from home thou dost not fly, Home -
Frem - de sein, Und bleibst du auch im Va - ter - haus, Wirst
I am gone, For tho' from home thou dost not fly,
Frem - de sein, Und bleibst du auch im Va - ter - haus,
I am gone, For tho' from home thou dost not fly,
Frem - de sein, Und bleibst du auch im Va - ter - haus,
I am gone, For tho' from home thou dost not fly,
Frem - de sein, Und bleibst du auch im Va - ter - haus,
25
attacca
- joys are fled, when I am gone.
doch wie in der Frem - de sein.
Home - joys are fled, when I am gone.
Wirst doch wie in der Frem - de sein.
Home - joys are fled, when I am gone.
Wirst doch wie in der Frem - de sein.
Home - joys are fled, when I am gone.
Wirst doch wie in der Frem - de sein.

Un poco allegro

39
cresc.
fled from __ home on a night in __ May, And none ev - er
flo - hen __ heim - lich von Hau - se __ fort, Es wusst' we - der
cresc.
fled from __ home on a night in __ May, And none ev - er
flo - hen __ heim - lich von Hau - se __ fort, Es wusst' we - der
cresc.
fled from __ home on a night in __ May, And none ev - er
flo - hen __ heim - lich von Hau - se __ fort, Es wusst' we - der
cresc.
And none ev - er
Es wusst' we - der
42
f p p
knew, __ none ev - er knew of their go - ing. They wan - der'd wide o'er the
Va - ter, we - der Va - ter noch Mut - ter. Sie sind ge - wan - dert __
f p p
knew of their go - ing. They wan - der'd wide o'er the
Va - ter noch Mut - ter. Sie sind ge - wan - dert
f p p
knew, __ none ev - er knew of their go - ing. They wan - der'd wide o'er the
Va - ter, we - der Va - ter noch Mut - ter. Sie sind ge - wan - dert
f p p
knew of their go - ing. They wan - der'd wide o'er the
Va - ter noch Mut - ter. Sie sind ge - wan - dert
46
world a - far, But ne - ver be - held for - tune's gui - ding __ star, In
hin und her, Sie ha - ben ge - habt we - der Glück noch __ Stern, Sie
world a - far, But ne - ver be - held for - tune's gui - ding __ star, In
hin und her, Sie ha - ben ge - habt we - der Glück noch __ Stern, Sie
world a - far, But ne - ver be - held for - tune's gui - ding __ star, In
hin und her, Sie ha - ben ge - habt we - der Glück noch __ Stern, Sie
world a - far, In
hin und her, Sie

49
cresc.
f
p
rit.
blight and sor - row, in sor - row they end - ed.
sind ge - stor - ben, ge - stor - ben, ver - dor - ben.
blight and sor - row they end - - - - ed.
sind ge - stor - ben, ver - dor - - - - ben.
blight and sor - row, in sor - row they end - ed.
sind ge - stor - ben, ge - stor - ben, ver - dor - ben.
blight and sor - row they end - - - - ed.
sind ge - stor - ben, ver - dor - - - - ben.
PART III: Over their grave /Auf ihrem Grab
Assai sostenuto
53
mf
O - ver their grave the lin - den is grow - ing, The birds sweet - ly
Auf ih - rem Grab da steht ei - ne Lin - de, Drin pfei - fen die
O - ver their grave the lin - den is grow - ing,
Auf ih - rem Grab da steht ei - ne Lin - de,
55
sing - ing, and the soft winds blow - ing, While on the green - sward be - neath its
Vö - gel und A - bend - win - de, Und drun - ter sitzt auf dem grü - nen
While on the green - sward be - neath its
Und drun - ter sitzt auf dem grü - nen

58
dim.
p
cresc.
shade Sit vil - lage swain and ro - sy maid, While on the
Platz Der Mül - lers - knecht mit sei - nem Schatz, Und drun - ter
shade Sit vil - lage swain and ro - sy maid, While on the
Platz Der Mül - lers - knecht mit sei - nem Schatz, Und drun - ter
shade Sit vil - lage swain and ro - sy maid, While on the
Platz Der Mül - lers - knecht mit sei - nem Schatz, Und drun - ter
shade Sit vil - lage swain and ro - sy maid, While on the
Platz Der Mül - lers - knecht mit sei - nem Schatz, Und drun - ter
61
green-sward be - neath its shade Sit vil - lage swain and ro - sy maid.
sitzt auf dem grü - nen Platz Der Mül - lers - knecht mit sei - nem Schatz.
green-sward be-neath its shade Sit vil - lage swain and ro - sy maid.
sitzt auf dem grü - nen Platz Der Mül - lers - knecht mit sei - nem Schatz.
green - sward be-neath its shade Sit vil - lage swain and ro - sy maid.
sitzt auf dem grü - nen Platz Der Mül - lers - knecht mit sei - nem Schatz.
green - sward be-neath its shade Sit vil - lage swain and ro - sy maid.
sitzt auf dem grü - nen Platz Der Mül - lers - knecht mit sei - nem Schatz.
mf
65
The soft low winds in sad - ness are sigh - ing, The birds' faint
Die Win - de weh'n so still und so schau - rig, Die Vö - gel
The soft low winds in sad - ness are sigh - ing, The birds' faint
Die Win - de weh'n so still und so schau - rig, Die Vö - gel
The soft low winds in sad - ness are sigh - ing, The birds' faint
Die Win - de weh'n so still und so schau - rig, Die Vö - gel
The soft low winds in sad - ness are sigh - ing,
Die Win - de weh'n so still und so schau - rig,

67
cresc.
notes_ with the day - light are dy - ing; The maid and her swain list - en si - lent -
sin - gen so süss_ und so trau - rig, Die schwa - tzen - den Buh - len, sie wer - den
cresc.
notes_ with the day - light are dy - ing; The maid and her swain list - en si - lent -
sin - gen so süss_ und so trau - rig, Die schwa - tzen - den Buh - len, sie wer - den
cresc.
notes with the day - light are dy - ing; The maid_ and her swain list - en si - lent -
sin - gen so süss und so trau - rig, Die schwa - tzen - den Buh - len, sie wer - den
p cresc.
The maid and her swain list - en si - lent -
Die schwa - tzen - den Buh - len, sie wer - den
70
dim. p cresc.
- ly, And weep, but they weep with - out know - ing why, The maid and her
stumm, Sie wei - nen und wis - sen selbst nicht wa - rum, Die schwa - tzen - den
dim. p cresc.
- ly, And weep, but they weep with - out know - ing why, The maid and her
stumm, Sie wei - nen und wis - sen selbst nicht wa - rum, Die schwa - tzen - den
dim. p cresc.
- ly, And weep, but they weep with - out know - ing why, The maid_ and her
stumm, Sie wei - nen und wis - sen selbst nicht wa - rum, Die schwa - tzen - den
dim. p cresc.
- ly, And weep, but they weep with - out know - ing why, The maid and her
stumm, Sie wei - nen und wis - sen selbst nicht wa - rum, Die schwa - tzen - den
73
p pp
swain list - en si - lent - ly, And weep, but they weep with - out know - ing why.
Buh - len, sie wer - den_ stumm, Sie wei - nen und wis - sen selbst nicht wa - rum.
p pp
swain list - en si - lent - ly, And weep, but they weep with - out know - ing why.
Buh - len, sie wer - den stumm, Sie wei - nen und wis - sen selbst nicht wa - rum.
p pp
swain list - en si - lent - ly, And weep, but they weep with - out know - ing why.
Buh - len, sie wer - den stumm, Sie wei - nen und wis - sen selbst nicht wa - rum.
p pp
swain list - en si - lent - ly, And weep, but they weep with - out know - ing why.
Buh - len, sie wer - den stumm, Sie wei - nen und wis - sen selbst nicht wa - rum.

12. Departure

Abschied vom Walde

JOSEPH VON EICHENDORFF
tr. W. BARTHOLOMEW

FELIX MENDELSSOHN
Op. 59 No. 3

8
cresc.
f
breast. When far from you I wan - der, Learn - ing the world is
halt! Da drau - ssen, stets be - tro - gen, Saust die ge-schäft'-ge
cresc.
f
breast. When far from you I wan - der, Learn - ing the world is
halt! Da drau - ssen, stets be - tro - gen, Saust die ge-schäft'-ge
cresc.
f
breast. When far from you I wan - der, Learn - ing the world is
halt! Da drau - ssen, stets be - tro - gen, Saust die ge-schäft'-ge
cresc.
f
breast. When far from you I wan - der, Learn - ing the world is
halt! Da drau - ssen, stets be - tro - gen, Saust die ge-schäft'-ge
12
pp
vain, My heart will fond - ly pon - der, And sigh for you a -
Welt; Schlag' noch ein - mal die Bo - gen Um mich, du grü - nes
pp
vain, My heart will fond - ly pon - der, And sigh for you a -
Welt; Schlag' noch ein - mal die Bo - gen Um mich, du grü - nes
pp
vain, My heart will fond - ly pon - der, And sigh for you a -
Welt; Schlag' noch ein - mal die Bo - gen Um mich, du grü - nes
pp
vain, My heart will fond - ly pon - der, my
Welt; Schlag' noch ein - mal die Bo - gen, schlag'
16
f
dim.
p
- gain, My heart will fond - ly pon - der, And sigh for
Zelt, Schlag' noch ein - mal die Bo - gen Um mich, du
f
dim.
- gain, My heart will fond - ly pon - der, And sigh
Zelt, Schlag' noch ein - mal die Bo - gen Um mich,
f
dim.
p
- gain, My heart will fond - ly pon - der, And sigh for
Zelt, Schlag' noch ein - mal die Bo - gen Um mich, du
cresc.
sf
f
dim.
p
heart will fond - ly pon - der, And sigh for
noch ein - mal die Bo - gen Um mich, du

20
p
you a - gain! In sha - dy glens re - cli - ning, I
grü - nes Zelt! Im Wal - de steht ge - schrie - ben Ein
p p
for you a - gain! In sha - dy glens re - cli - ning, I
du grü - nes Zelt! Im Wal - de steht ge - schrie - ben Ein
p
you a - gain! In sha - dy glens re - cli - ning, I
grü - nes Zelt! Im Wal - de steht ge - schrie - ben Ein
p
you a - gain! In sha - dy glens re - cli - ning, I
grü - nes Zelt! Im Wal - de steht ge - schrie - ben Ein
24
f p
trace the wrong and right; The beam of rea - son shi - ning, Shows
stil - les ern - stes Wort Vom rech - ten Thun und Lie - ben, Und
f p
trace the wrong and right; The beam of rea - son shi - ning, Shows
stil - les ern - stes Wort Vom rech - ten Thun und Lie - ben, Und
f p
trace the wrong and right; The beam of rea - son shi - ning, Shows
stil - les ern - stes Wort Vom rech - ten Thun und Lie - ben, Und
f p
trace the wrong and right; The beam of rea - son shi - ning, Shows
stil - les ern - stes Wort Vom rech - ten Thun und Lie - ben, Und
28
cresc.
Vir - tue ev - er bright. The book I read is Na - ture's;
was des Men - schen Hort. Ich ha - be treu ge - le - sen
cresc.
Vir - tue ev - er bright. The book I read is Na - ture's;
was des Men - schen Hort. Ich ha - be treu ge - le - sen
cresc.
Vir - tue ev - er bright. The book I read is Na - ture's;
was des Men - schen Hort. Ich ha - be treu ge - le - sen
cresc.
Vir - tue ev - er bright. The book I read is Na - ture's;
was des Men - schen Hort. Ich ha - be treu ge - le - sen

32
f
pp
There sim - ple truths ap - pear, And tho' she change
Die Wor - te, schlicht und wahr, Und durch mein gan - zes
There sim - ple truths ap - pear, And tho' she change her
Die Wor - te, schlicht und wahr, Und durch mein gan - zes
8
There sim - ple truths ap - pear, And tho' she change her
Die Wor - te, schlicht und wahr, Und durch mein gan - zes
There sim - ple truths ap - pear, And tho' she change her
Die Wor - te, schlicht und wahr, Und durch mein gan - zes
35
fea - tures, Her dic - tates still are clear, And
We - sen Ward's un - aus - sprech - lich klar, Und
fea - tures, Her dic - tates still are clear, And
We - sen Ward's un - aus - sprech - lich klar, Und
fea - tures, Her dic - tates still are clear, And
We - sen Ward's un - aus - sprech - lich klar, Und
cresc.
sf
fea - - - - tures, and tho' she change her
We - - - - sen, und durch mein gan - zes
38
dim.
p
tho' she change her fea - tures, Her dic - tates
durch mein gan - zes We - sen Ward's un - aus -
tho' she change her fea - tures, Her dic - - - -
durch mein gan - zes We - sen Ward's un - - - -
tho' she change her fea - tures, Her dic - tates
durch mein gan - zes We - sen Ward's un - aus -
fea - - - - - - tures, Her dic - tates
We - - - - - - sen Ward's un - aus -

41
p
still are clear. Yet must I now be - take me To
- sprech - lich klar. Bald werd' ich dich ver - las - sen, Fremd
- - tates still are clear. Yet must I now be - take me To
- - aus - sprech - lich klar. Bald werd' ich dich ver - las - sen, Fremd
still are clear. Yet must I now be - take me To
- sprech - - lich klar. Bald werd' ich dich ver - las - sen, Fremd
still are clear. Yet must I now be - take me To
- sprech - - lich klar. Bald werd' ich dich ver - las - sen, Fremd
45
f
scenes of toil and strife, Ah! why does For - tune make me Still
in die Frem - de geh'n, Auf bunt - be - weg - ten Gas - sen Des
scenes of toil and strife, Ah! why does For - tune make me Still
in die Frem - de geh'n, Auf bunt - be - weg - ten Gas - sen Des
scenes of toil and strife, Ah! why does For - tune make me Still
in die Frem - de geh'n, Auf bunt - be - weg - ten Gas - sen Des
scenes of toil and strife, Ah! why does For - tune make me Still
in die Frem - de geh'n, Auf bunt - be - weg - ten Gas - sen Des
49
cresc.
play the farce of life? Tho' call'd from you by du - ty,
Le - bens Schau - spiel seh'n. Und mit - ten in dem Le - ben
play the farce of life? Tho' call'd from you by du - ty,
Le - bens Schau - spiel seh'n. Und mit - ten in dem Le - ben
play the farce of life? Tho' call'd from you by du - ty,
Le - bens Schau - spiel seh'n. Und mit - ten in dem Le - ben
play the farce of life? Tho' call'd from you by du - ty,
Le - bens Schau - spiel seh'n. Und mit - ten in dem Le - ben

53

f Still, where - so - e'er I stray, The thought of all your
Wird dei - nes Ernst's Ge - walt Mich Ein - sa - men er -

f Still, where - so - e'er I stray, The thought of all your
Wird dei - nes Ernst's Ge - walt Mich Ein - sa - men er -

f Still, where - so - e'er I stray, The thought of all your
Wird dei - nes Ernst's Ge - walt Mich Ein - sa - men er -

f Still, where - so - e'er I stray, The thought of all your
Wird dei - nes Ernst's Ge - walt Mich Ein - sa - men er -

56

beau - ty Will ne - ver fade a - way, The thought of all your
- he - ben, So wird mein Herz nicht alt, Mich Ein - sa - men er -

beau - ty Will ne - ver fade a - way, The thought of all your
- he - ben, So wird mein Herz nicht alt, Mich Ein - sa - men er -

beau - ty Will ne - ver fade a - way, The thought of all your
- he - ben, So wird mein Herz nicht alt, Mich Ein - sa - men er -

beau - - ty, the thought of all your beau - -
- he - - ben, mich Ein - sa - men er - he - -

60

beau - ty Will ne - ver fade a - way.
- he - ben, So wird mein Herz nicht alt.

beau - ty Will ne - - - ver fade a - way.
- he - ben, So wird mein Herz nicht alt.

beau - ty Will ne - ver fade a - way.
- he - ben, So wird mein Herz nicht alt.

- ty Will ne - ver fade a - way.
- ben, So wird mein Herz nicht alt.

13. Orpheus, with his lute

WILLIAM SHAKESPEARE — GEORGE MACFARREN

13
trees and moun - tains Bow them - selves when he did sing; To his
made moun - tains Bow when he did sing; To his
trees and moun - tains Bow them - selves when he did sing; To his
dim.
made trees Bow when he did sing; To his
17
mu - sic plants and flow - ers, plants and flow - ers Ev - er sprung,
mu - sic plants and flow - ers, plants and flow - ers Ev - er sprung, as
mu - sic plants and flow - ers, plants and flow - ers Ev - er sprung,
mu - sic plants and flow - ers, plants and flow - ers Ev - er sprung,
21
as sun and show - ers There had made a last - ing spring;
sun and show - ers There had made a last - ing spring;
as sun and show - ers There had made a last - ing spring;
There had made a last - ing spring;

25
p
E - ve - ry thing that heard him play, e - ve - ry thing that heard him play,
p
E - ve - ry thing that heard him play, e - ve - ry thing that heard him play,
p
E - ve - ry thing that heard him play, e - ve - ry thing that heard him play,
p
e - ve - ry thing that heard him play,
29
pp
Ev - en the bil - lows of the sea, ev - en the bil - lows of the sea
cresc.
[pp]
Ev - en the bil - lows of the sea
cresc.
pp
Ev - en the bil - lows of the sea, ev - en the bil - lows
cresc.
pp
Ev - en the bil - lows of the sea
cresc.
33
sf p
Hung their heads and then lay by, hung their heads and then lay
dim.
sf p
Hung their heads and then lay by, hung their heads and then lay
dim.
sf p
Hung their heads and then lay by, hung their heads and then lay
dim.
sf p
Hung their heads and then lay by, hung their heads and then lay
dim.

37
pp
cresc.
by. In sweet mu - sic, in sweet mu - sic, in sweet mu - sic is such
by. In sweet mu - sic, in sweet mu - sic, in sweet mu - sic is such
by. In sweet mu - sic, in sweet mu - sic, in sweet mu - sic is such
by. In sweet mu - sic, in sweet mu - sic, in sweet mu - sic is such
41
ff dim.
poco rit.
a tempo
p
art, in sweet mu - sic is such
art, in sweet mu - sic is such
ff
art, in sweet mu - - sic, in sweet mu - sic is such
art, in sweet mu - sic is such
46
f
p
art, in mu - sic is such art, Kill - ing care and
art, in mu - sic is such art, Kill - ing care and
art, in mu - sic is such art, Kill - ing care and
art, in mu - sic is such art,

50
pp cresc.
grief of heart, and grief of heart. Fall a-sleep,
pp [cresc.]
grief of heart, and grief of heart. Fall a-sleep,
pp [cresc.]
grief of heart, and grief of heart. Fall a-sleep,
pp [cresc.]
Fall a-sleep, fall a-
54
f dim.
fall a-sleep, or, hear-ing, die, or, hear-ing,
f [dim.]
fall a-sleep, or, hear-ing, die, or, hear-ing,
f [dim.]
fall a-sleep, or, hear-ing, die, or, hear-ing,
f [mf]
-sleep, or, hear-ing, die, or,
58
p
die, or, hear-ing, die, or, hear-ing,
p
die, or, hear-ing, die, fall a-sleep, or, hear-ing,
p
die, or, hear-ing, die, fall a-sleep, or, hear-ing,
[dim.] p
hear ing, or, hear-ing, die, or, hear-ing,

62
pp
die, or, hear - ing, die, fall a - sleep,
die, or, hear - ing, die, fall a - sleep, fall a -
8
die, or, hear - ing, die, fall a - sleep,
die, or, hear - ing, die, fall a - sleep, fall a -
67
sempre decresc.
fall a - sleep, fall a - sleep, or, hear - ing,
[sempre decresc.]
- sleep, fall a - sleep, or, hear - ing,
fall a - sleep, fall a - sleep, or, hear - ing,
- sleep,
72
hear - ing, die.
hear - ing, die.
hear - ing, die.
hear - ing, die.

14. When daisies pied

WILLIAM SHAKESPEARE

GEORGE MACFARREN

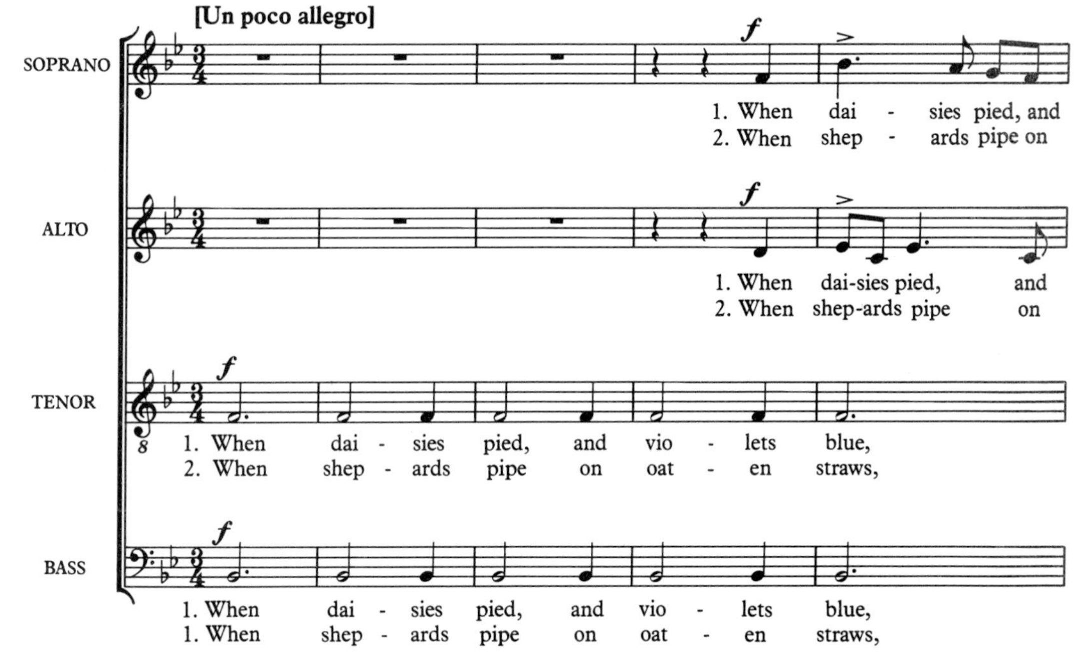

[Un poco allegro]

SOPRANO

f

1. When dai - sies pied, and
2. When shep - ards pipe on

ALTO

f

1. When dai-sies pied, and
2. When shep-ards pipe on

TENOR

f

1. When dai - sies pied, and vio - lets blue,
2. When shep - ards pipe on oat - en straws,

BASS

f

1. When dai - sies pied, and vio - lets blue,
1. When shep - ards pipe on oat - en straws,

9
cu - ckoo - buds of yel - low hue, Do paint the mea - dows with de -
tur - tles tread, and rooks, and daws, And maid - ens bleach their sum - mer
cu - ckoo - buds of yel - low hue, Do paint the mea - dows with de -
tur - tles tread, and rooks, and daws, And maid - ens bleach their sum - mer
And cu - ckoo - buds, Do paint the mea - dows with de -
When tur - tles tread, And maid - ens bleach their sum - mer
And cu - ckoo - buds, Do paint the mea - dows with de -
When tur - tles tread, And maid - ens bleach their sum - mer
12
pp
- light, When dai - sies pied, and vio - lets blue, And
smocks, When shep - ards pipe on oat - en straws, And
pp
- light, When dai - sies pied, and vio - lets blue, And
smocks, When shep - ards pipe on oat - en straws, And
pp
- light, When dai - sies pied, And
smocks, When shep - ards pipe, And
pp
- light, When dai - sies pied, And
smocks, When shep - ards pipe, And
15
la - dy - smocks all sil - ver - white, And cu - ckoo - buds of yel - low
mer - ry larks are plough - man's clocks, When tur - tles tread, and rooks, and
la - dy - smocks all sil - ver - white, And cu - ckoo - buds of yel - low
mer - ry larks are plough - man's clocks, When tur - tles tread, and rooks, and
la - dy - smocks all sil - ver - white, And
mer - ry larks are plough - man's clocks, When
la - dy - smocks all sil - ver - white, And
mer - ry larks are plough - man's clocks, When

18
cresc.
hue, Do paint the mea - dows with de - light, The cu - ckoo then, on
daws, And maid-ens bleach their sum-mer smocks,
cu - ckoo-buds, Do paint the mea - dows with de - light, The cu - ckoo then, on
tur - tles tread, And maid-ens bleach their sum-mer smocks,
22
f
p
ev' - ry tree, Mocks mar - ried men,
for thus sings he, for thus sings
for thus
26
Cu - ckoo, cu - ckoo,
he, for thus sings he, thus sings he,
[cresc.]
sings he, for thus sings he, thus sings he,

31
cu - ckoo, cu - ckoo, cu - ckoo, cu - ckoo,
pp cresc.
O word of fear, O word of fear, O
37
cu - ckoo, cu - ckoo, cu - ckoo, cu - ckoo,
f sf dim. pp cresc.
word un - pleas - ing to a mar - ried ear, O word of fear,
43
cu - ckoo, cu - ckoo, Word of fear, un-pleas-ing to a mar - ried ear!
f sf ff
O word of fear, O word of fear, un-pleas-ing to a mar - ried ear!

15. Come live with me

CHRISTOPHER MARLOWE

WILLIAM STERNDALE BENNETT

9
dim.
p
crag - gy moun - tains yield. There will we sit up - on the
crag - gy moun - tains yield. There will we sit up - on the
crag - gy moun - tains yield. There will we sit up - on the
crag - gy moun - tains yield. There will we
12
calando
rocks, And see the shep - herds feed their flocks, By shal - low
rocks, And see the shep - herds feed their flocks, By shal - low
rocks, And see the shep-herds feed their flocks, By shal - low
sit up - on the rocks, By shal - low
15
sempre
pp
ri - vers, to whose falls Me - lo - dious birds sing
ri - vers, to whose falls Me - lo - dious birds sing
ri - vers, to whose falls Me - lo - dious birds sing ma - dri -
ri - vers, to whose falls Me - lo - dious birds sing

18
f
ma - dri - gals, And if these plea - sures may thee move, Then live with
ma - dri - gals, And if these plea - sures may thee move, Then live with
8 - gals, And if these plea - sures may thee move, Then live with
ma - dri - gals, And if these plea - sures may thee move, Then live with
21
ff
me, and be my love, And if these plea - sures may thee
me, and be my love, And if these plea - sures may thee
8 me, and be my love, And if these plea - sures may thee
me, and be my love, And if these plea - sures may thee
24
dim.
p
move, Then live with me, and be my love, then live with
move, Then live with me, and be my love,
8 move, Then live with me, and be my love,
move, Then live with me, and be my love, then

27
me, and be my
f
then live with me, and be my
f
then live with me, and be my
f
live, then live, then live with me, and be my
30
love, then live with me,
[>]
love, then live with me,
[>]
love, then live with me,
love, then live with me, then live with
33
and be my love. There will I make thee beds of
f
and be my love. There will I make thee beds of
f
and be my love. There will I make thee beds of
f
me, and be my love. There will I make thee beds of

36
ro - ses, With a thou - sand fra - grant po - sies, A cap of
ro - ses, With a thou - sand fra - grant po - sies, A cap of
ro - ses, With a thou - sand fra - grant po - sies, A cap of
ro - ses, With a thou - sand fra - grant po - sies, A cap of
39
flow - ers, and a kir - tle, a cap of flow - ers, and a
flow - ers, and a kir - tle, cap of flow - ers, and a
flow - ers, and a kir - tle, cap of flow - ers, and a
flow - ers, and a kir - tle, cap of flow - ers, and a
42
dim.
p
kir - tle Em - broi - der'd all with leaves of myr - tle, The
kir - tle Em - broi - der'd all with leaves of myr - tle, The
kir - tle Em - broi - der'd all with leaves of myr - tle, The shep - herd
kir - tle Em - broi - der'd all with leaves of myr - tle, The

45
shep - herd swains shall dance and sing For thy de -
shep - herd swains shall dance and sing For thy de -
swains shall dance and sing For thy de -
shep - - - herd swains shall
47
calando
- light, each May morn - ing, The shep - herd
- light, each May morn - ing, The shep - herd
- light, each May morn - ing, The shep - herd
dance and sing, the shep - - herd
49
sempre
[p]
pp
swains shall dance and sing For thy de - light, each
swains shall dance and sing For thy de - light, each
swains shall dance and sing For thy de - light, each May morn -
swains shall sing For thy de - light, each

52
May morn - ing; If these de - lights thy mind may
May morn - ing; If these de - lights thy mind may
- ing; If these de - lights thy mind may
May morn - ing; If these de - lights thy mind may
54
move, Then live with me, and be my love, If these de -
move, Then live with me, and be my love, If these de -
move, Then live with me, and be my love, If these de -
move, Then live with me, and be my love, If these de -
57
- lights thy mind may move, Then live with me, and be my
- lights thy mind may move, Then live with me, and
- lights thy mind may move, Then live with me, and
- lights thy mind may move, Then live with me, and
f
ff
dim.
p

60
love, then live with me,
be my love, then live with me,
be my love, then live with me,
be my love, then live, then live, then live with
63
and be my love, then live with me,
and be my love, then live with me,
and be my love,
me, and be my love, then live with
66
and be my love.
and be my love.
then live with me, and be my love.
me, then live with me, and be my love.

16. Sweet Stream that winds through yonder glade

WILLIAM COWPER

WILLIAM STERNDALE BENNETT

11
(tranquillo)
em - blem, em - - - blem of a vir - tuous
em - - - - - - blem of a vir - tuous
delicato
sweet Stream that winds through yon - der glade, through yon - der
em - blem, apt em - - - blem of a vir - tuous
14
p
(espress.)
maid, Si - lent and chaste, she steals a -
maid, she steals a - long,
glade, she steals a - long,
maid, she steals a - long,
18
sf
cresc.
p [tranquillo]
- long, Far from the world's gay bu - sy throng, Si - lent and
she steals a - long, Far from the world's gay bu - sy throng, Si -
she steals a - long, Far from the world's gay bu - sy throng, Si -
she steals a - long, Far from the world's gay bu - sy throng,

22
pp
chaste, si - lent and chaste, she steals a - long, she steals a -
- lent, si - lent and chaste, she steals a - long, she steals a -
- lent, si - lent and chaste, and chaste, she steals a -
p [tranquillo]
Si - lent and chaste, she steals a - long, she steals a -
25
sf
cresc.
dim.
p
- long, Far from the world's, the world's gay bu - sy throng; With
28
gen - tle yet pre - vail - ing force, In - tent, in -
gen - tle yet pre - vail - ing force, In -
gen - tle, gen - tle force, In -

30
sf
- tent up - on her des - tin'd course, in - tent up -
sf
- tent up - on her des - tin'd course, in - tent up -
[sf]
- tent up - on her course, in - tent up -
[sf]
- tent up - on her course, in - tent up -
p
32
- on her des - tin'd course, in - tent up - on her des - tin'd
- on her des - tin'd course, in - tent up - on her des - tin'd
- on her des - tin'd course, in - tent up - on her des - tin'd
- on her des - tin'd course, in - tent up - on her des - tin'd
cresc.
35
course, in - tent up - on her des - tin'd course, Sweet
course, in - tent up - on her des - tin'd course, Sweet
course, in - tent up - on her des - tin'd course, Sweet
course, in - tent up - on her des - tin'd course, Sweet
dim. espress.
p
pp

38
p
Stream, apt emblem, Grace - ful and use - ful all she
Stream, apt em - blem, Grace - ful and use - ful all she
Stream, apt em - blem, Grace - ful and use - ful all she
Stream, apt em - blem, Grace - -
41
sf
cresc.
does, Bless - ing and blest, and blest where - 'er she
does, Bless - - ing and blest, and blest where - 'er she
does, Bless - - ing and blest, and blest, and
- ful, Bless - - ing and blest, and blest, and
44
pp
(tranquillo assai)
goes, Pure bo - som'd as that wa - t'ry glass, And
goes, Pure bo - som'd as that wa - t'ry glass, And
blest, Pure bo - som'd as that wa - t'ry glass, And
blest, Pure bo - som'd as that wa - t'ry glass, And

47
f
heav'n re - flec - ted, heav'n re - flec - ted, re -
f
heav'n re - flec - ted, heav'n re - flec - ted, re -
f
heav'n re - flec - ted, heav'n re - flec - ted, re -
f
heav'n re - flec - ted, heav'n re - flec - ted, re -
50
dim. espress.
pp
- flec - ted in her face, Bless-ing and blest where - 'er she
dim. espress.
pp
- flec - ted in her face, Bless-ing and blest where - 'er she
dim. espress.
pp
- flec - ted in her face, Bless-ing and blest where - 'er she
dim. espress.
pp
- flec - ted in her face, Bless-ing and blest where - 'er she
53
espress. sostenuto
cresc.
goes, Pure bo - som'd as that wa - t'ry glass, And heav'n
espress. sostenuto
cresc.
goes, Pure bo - som'd as that wa - t'ry glass, And heav'n
espress. sostenuto
cresc.
goes, Pure as that wa - t'ry glass, And heav'n
espress. sostenuto
cresc.
goes, Pure as that wa - t'ry glass, And heav'n

56
sf
dim.
re - flec - - ted, heav'n, and heav'n re -
dim.
re - flec - ted, and heav'n re -
dim.
re - flec - ted, heav'n, and heav'n re -
dim.
re - flec - ted, and heav'n re -
59
p
rall.
- flec - ted, re - flec - ted, re - flec - ted in her
p
- flec - ted, re - flec - ted, re - flec - ted in her
p
- flec - ted, re - flec - ted, re - flec - ted in her
[p]
- flec - ted, re - flec - ted in her
62
pp
face. Sweet Stream, sweet Stream, sweet Stream.
pp
face. Sweet Stream, sweet Stream, sweet Stream, sweet Stream.
pp
face. Sweet Stream, sweet Stream, sweet Stream, sweet Stream.
pp
face. Sweet Stream, sweet Stream, sweet Stream.

17. Sweet and low

LULLABY

ALFRED, LORD TENNYSON

JOSEPH BARNBY

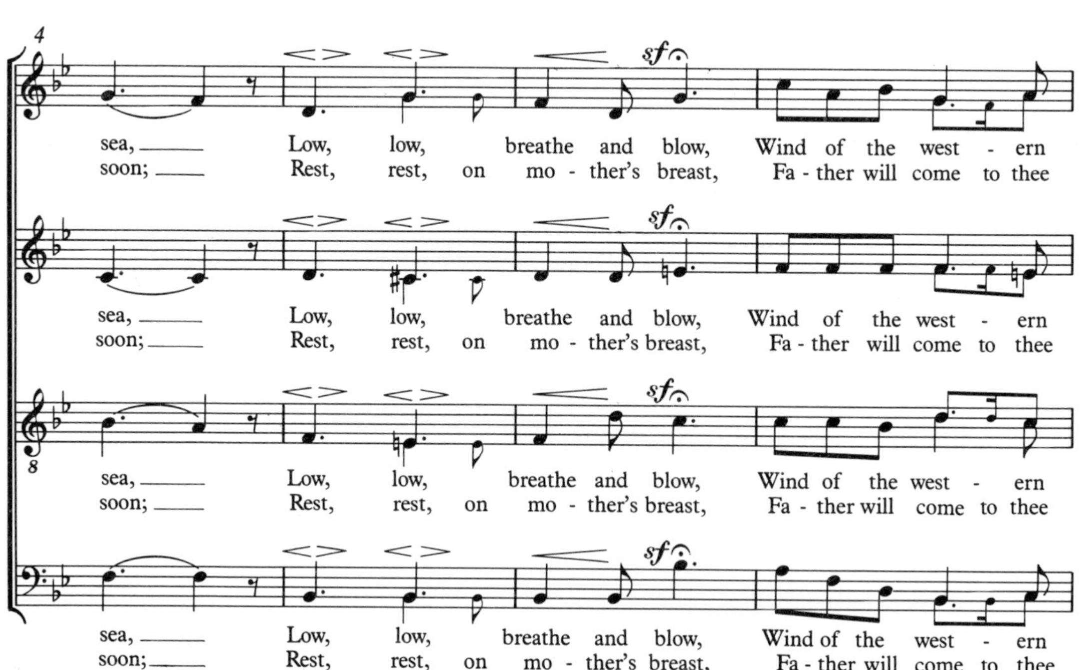

8
mf
sea! Ov - er the roll - ing wa - ters go,
soon; Fa - ther will come to his babe in the nest,
sea! Ov - er the wa - ters go,
soon; Fa - ther, his babe in the nest,
11
pp
f
Come from the dy - ing moon, and blow, Blow him a - gain to me,
Sil - ver sails all out of the west Un - der the sil - ver moon!
Come from the moon, and blow, Blow him a - gain to me,
Sil - ver sails out of the west Un - der the sil - ver moon!
15
p
rall. e dim.
pp
While my lit - tle one, while my pret - ty one, sleeps.
Sleep, my lit - tle one, sleep my pret - ty one, sleep.

18. O hush thee, my babie

SIR WALTER SCOTT

ARTHUR SULLIVAN

15
cresc.
f
all be - long - ing, dear ba - bie, to thee, they are all be -
They are all be - long - ing to thee, they are all be -
They are all be - long - ing to thee, they are all be -
They are all be - long - ing to thee, they are all be -
20
[dim.]
p
pp
stacc.
pp stacc.
- long - ing, dear ba - bie, to thee. O
- long - ing, dear ba - bie, to thee. O hush thee, my ba - bie, O
- long - ing, dear ba - bie, to thee. O hush thee, my ba - bie, O
- long - ing to thee. O hush thee, O hush thee, my ba - bie, O
25
hush thee, my ba - - - - - bie.
hush thee, my ba - bie, O hush thee, my ba - - bie.
hush thee, my ba - bie, O hush thee, my ba - - bie.
hush thee, my ba - bie, O hush thee, my ba - - bie.

f
31
O fear not the bugle, though loudly it blows; It
O fear not the bugle, though loudly it blows; It
O fear not the bugle, though loudly it blows; It
O fear not the bugle, though loudly it blows; It
35
cresc.
dim.
calls but the wards-ers that guard thy re-pose, that guard thy re-
calls but the wards-ers that guard thy re-pose, that guard thy re-
calls but the wards-ers that guard thy re-pose, that guard thy re-
calls but the wards-ers that guard thy re-pose, that guard thy re-
40
-pose. Their bows would be bend-ed, their blades would be red, Ere the
-pose. Their bows would be bend-ed, their blades would be red,
-pose. Their bows would be bend-ed, their blades would be red,
-pose. Their bows would be bend-ed, their blades would be red,

45
cresc.
f
step of a foe - man draws near to thy bed, ere the step of a
Ere the step of a foe - man draws near, ere the step of a
Ere the step of a foe - man draws near, ere the step of a
Ere the step of a foe - man draws near, ere the step of a
50
[dim.]
p
pp
stacc.
pp stacc.
foe - man draws near to thy bed. O
foe - man draws near to thy bed. O hush thee, my ba - bie, O
foe - man draws near to thy bed. O hush thee, my ba - bie, O
foe - man draws near. O hush thee, O hush thee, my ba - bie, O
55
hush thee, my ba - - - bie.
hush thee, my ba - bie, O hush thee, my ba - - bie.
hush thee, my ba - bie, O hush thee, my ba - - bie.
hush thee, my ba - bie, O hush thee, my ba - - bie.

61
p
O hush thee, my ba - bie, the time soon will come, When thy sleep shall be
66
bro - ken by trum - pet and drum, by trum - pet and drum. Then hush thee, my
bro - ken by trum - pet and drum, by trum - pet and drum. Then hush thee, my
72
dar - ling, take rest while you may, For strife comes with man - hood, and wa - king with
cresc.
dim.
For strife comes with man -

78
day, for strife comes with man - hood, and wa - king with day.
day, for strife comes with man - hood, and wa - king with day. O
8 - hood, for strife comes with man - hood, and wa - king with day. O
day, for strife comes with man - hood, and wa - king with day. O hush thee, O
84
O hush thee, O hush thee, O
hush thee, my ba - bie, O hush thee, my ba - bie, O hush thee, my ba - bie, O
hush thee, my ba - bie, O hush thee, my ba - bie, O hush thee, my ba - bie, O
hush thee, my ba - bie, O hush thee, my ba - bie, O hush thee, my ba - bie, O
90
hush thee, O hush thee, O hush thee, my ba - - bie!
hush thee, my babe, O hush thee, my ba - - bie!
hush thee, O hush thee, O hush thee, my ba - - bie!
hush thee, my babe, O hush thee, my ba - - bie!
stacc.
pp
p
dim.
rall.

19. Echoes

THOMAS MOORE

ARTHUR SULLIVAN

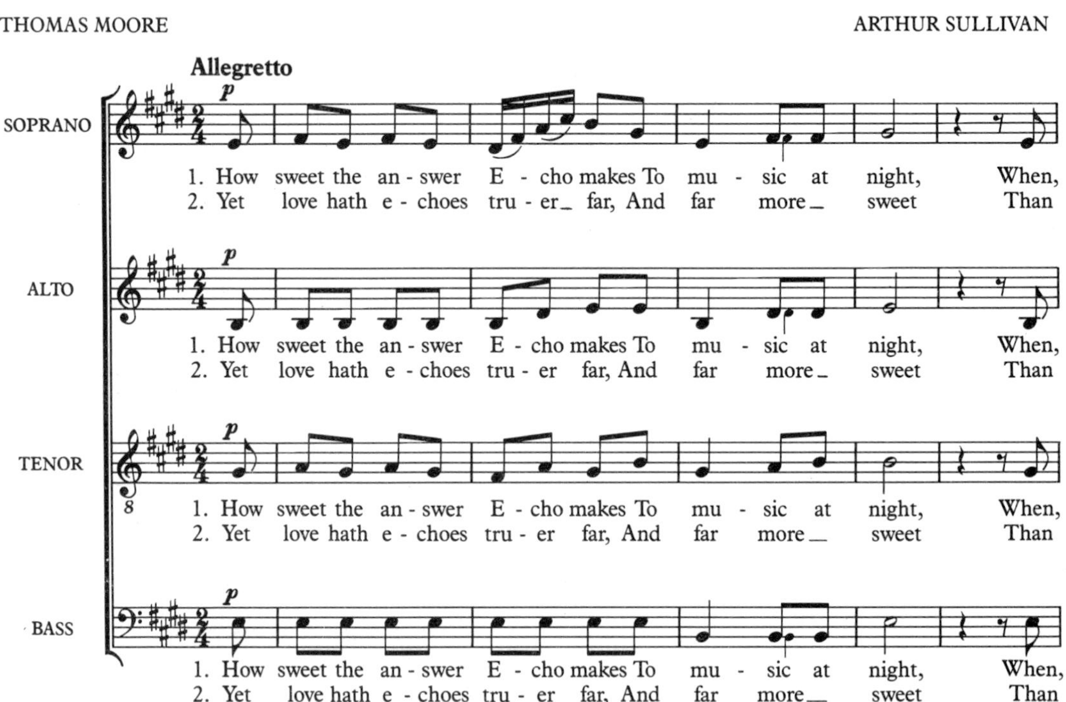

11
light, an - sw'ring light! How sweet the an - swer
- peat, the songs re - peat, Yet Love hath e- choes
- way o'er lawns and lakes Goes an - sw'ring light, goes an - sw'ring light! How sweet the an - swer
- peat, the songs re - peat, Yet Love hath e- choes
- way o'er lawns and lakes Goes an - sw'ring light! How sweet the an - swer
- peat, the songs re - peat, Yet Love hath e- choes
- way o'er lawns and lakes Goes an - sw'ring light, goes an-sw'ring light! How sweet the an - swer
- peat, re - peat, the songs re - peat, Yet Love hath e- choes
16
dim.
p
stacc.
E - cho makes To mu - sic at night, When, rous'd by lute or horn, she wakes, And,
tru - er far, And far more sweet, Than e'er be - neath the moon-light's star, Of
22
far a - way o'er lawns and lakes Goes an - sw'ring light, goes an - sw'ring light!
horn or lute or soft gui - tar The songs re - peat, the songs re - peat.

28
f
ff
3. 'Tis when the sigh in youth sin - cere, And on - ly then,
35
p
cresc.
The sigh that's breath'd for one to hear Is by that one, that on - ly Dear, Breath'd
The sigh that's breath'd for one to hear Is by that one, that on - ly Dear,
40
back a - gain, breath'd back a - gain, 'Tis when
Breath'd back a - gain, breath'd back a - gain, 'Tis when
Breath'd back a - gain, a- gain, breath'd back a - gain, 'Tis when

45
dim.
p
the sigh in youth sin - cere, And on - ly then, The
sigh that's breath'd for one to hear Is by that one, that on - ly Dear, is
50
stacc.
sigh that's breath'd for one to hear Is by that one, that on - ly Dear, is
54
pp
rall.
by that one, that on - ly Dear, Breath'd back a - gain, breath'd back a - gain.
by that one, that on - ly Dear, Breath'd back, breath'd back a - gain.

20. The long day closes

HENRY CHORLEY

ARTHUR SULLIVAN

* The small notes in the bass part are intended for use as *additional* notes, when the partsong is performed by a chorus.

18
Sit by the si - lent hearth In calm en - dea - vour, To count the sounds of
Sit by the si - lent hearth In calm en - dea - vour, To count the sounds of
Sit by the si - lent hearth In calm en - dea - vour, To count the sounds of
Sit by the si - lent hearth In calm en - dea - vour, To count the sounds of
24
mirth, Now dumb for ev - er. Heed not how hope be - lieves And fate dis -
mirth, Now dumb for ev - er. Heed not how hope be - lieves And fate dis -
mirth, Now dumb for ev - er. Heed not how hope be - lieves And fate dis -
mirth, Now dumb for ev - er. Heed not how hope be - lieves And fate dis -
29
- po - ses: Sha - dow is round the eaves, The long day clo - ses;
- po - ses: Sha - dow is round the eaves, The long day clo - ses;
- po - ses: Sha - dow is round the eaves, The long day clo - ses;
- po - ses: Sha - dow is round the eaves, The long day clo - ses; The

34
p
The light - ed win - dows dim
cresc.
Are fa - ding slow - ly. The
p
The light - ed win - dows dim
cresc.
Are fa - ding slow - ly. The
p
The light - ed win - dows dim
cresc.
Are fa - ding slow - ly. The
cresc.
light - ed win - dows dim Are fa - ding slow - ly. The fire that was so
39
dim.
pp
fire that was so trim Now quiv - ers _ low - ly, quiv - ers low - ly. Go to the dreamless
dim.
pp
fire that was so trim Now quiv - ers low - ly, quiv - ers low - ly. Go to the dreamless
dim.
pp
fire that was so trim Now quiv - ers _ low - ly, quiv - ers low - ly. Go to the dreamless
dim.
pp
trim Now quiv - ers low - ly, quiv - ers low - ly. Go to the dreamless
44
bed Where grief re - po - ses, Thy book of toil is read, The
bed Where grief re - po - ses, Thy book of toil is read, ___ The
bed Where grief re - po - ses, Thy book of toil is read, The
bed Where grief re - po - ses, Thy book of toil is read, The

49
f
long_ day clo - ses; Go to the dreamless bed Where grief re -
f
long_ day clo - ses; Go to the dreamless bed Where grief re -
f
long_ day clo - ses; Go ___ to the dreamless bed Where grief re -
f
long day clo - ses; Go to the dreamless bed Where grief re -
54
ff
dim.
- po - ses; Thy book of toil is read,_ thy book of toil is read,_
ff
dim.
- po - ses; Thy book of toil is read,_ thy book of toil is read,_
ff
dim.
- po - ses; Thy book of toil is read,_ thy book of toil is read,
ff
dim.
- po - ses; Thy book of toil is read, thy book of toil is read,___
59
p
pp
Go to the dream - less bed,___ The long day clo - ses.
p
pp
Go to the dream - less bed. The long day clo - ses.
p
pp
Go to the dream - less bed, The long day clo - ses.
p
pp
Go to the dream - less bed, The long day clo - ses.

21. There rolls the deep

ALFRED, LORD TENNYSON

C. HUBERT PARRY

13
hills are sha - dows, and they flow From form to
hills are sha - dows, and they flow From form to
hills are sha - dows, and they flow From form to
hills are sha - dows, and they flow From form to
16
cresc.
form, and no - thing stands; They melt like mist, the
form, and no - thing stands; They melt like mist, the
form, and no - thing stands; They melt like mist, the
form, and no - thing stands; They melt like mist, the
20
rit.
f
mf
so - lid lands, Like clouds they shape them-selves and go.
so - lid lands, Like clouds, like clouds they shape them-selves and go.
so - lid lands, Like clouds they shape them-selves and go.
so - lid lands, Like clouds, like clouds they shape them - selves and go.

a tempo
cresc.
But in my spi - rit will I dwell, And
But in my spi - rit will I dwell, And
But in my spi - rit will I dwell, And
But in my spi - rit will I dwell, And
dream my dream, and hold it true; For though my lips may
dream my dream, and hold it true; For though my lips may
dream my dream, and hold it true; For though my lips may
dream my dream, and hold it true; For though my lips may
poco animando
breathe a - dieu, I can - not think the thing fare -
breathe a - dieu, I can - not think the thing fare -
breathe a - dieu, I can - not think the thing fare -
breathe a - dieu, I can - not think the thing fare -

34
cresc.
-well, I can-not think the thing fare-well,
cresc.
-well, I can-not think the thing fare-well, I can-not think the
cresc.
8 -well, I can-not think the thing fare-well, I
cresc.
-well, I can-not think the thing fare-well, I
37
rit.
p
I can-not think the thing fare-well, I
p
thing, the thing fare-well, I
p
8 can - not think the thing fare-well, I
p
can - - not think, I can - not think the
40
p
pp
can-not think fare-well, fare-well, fare-well.
p
pp
can-not think fare-well, fare-well, fare-well.
p
pp
8 can-not think fare-well, fare-well, fare-well.
pp
thing fare-well, fare-well, fare-well.

22. Music, when soft voices die

10
rose is dead,_ Are heaped,_ are heaped for the be - lov - ed's bed; And
rose_ is dead,_ Are heaped, heaped for the be - lov - ed's bed;_ And
rose is dead,_ Are heaped,_ heaped for the be - lov - ed's bed;_ And
rose_ is dead, Are heaped, heaped for the be - lov - ed's bed; And
13
so_ thy_ thoughts,_ when thou art gone, Love_ it-self shall slum - ber, slum - ber,
so thy thoughts,_ when thou art gone,_ Love it - self_ shall slum - ber, slum - ber,
so thy thoughts,_ when thou_ art gone,_ Love it-self shall slum-ber, slum-ber,
so thy thoughts, when thou art gone, Love it - self_ shall slum-ber, slum-ber,
17
rit.
love_ it-self_ shall slum - ber on, love_ it-self shall slum - ber on.
love it - self_ shall slum - ber on, love_ it-self shall slum - ber on.
love it - self_ shall slum - ber on, love_ it-self shall slum - ber on.
love it-self shall slum - ber on, shall slum - ber_ on.

23. Heraclitus

WILLIAM CORY

CHARLES VILLIERS STANFORD
Op. 110 No. 4

12
f
I Had tired the sun with talk - ing and
p
[f]
you and I Had tired the sun with talk - ing and
p
f
you and I Had tired the sun with talk - ing and
p
f
you and I Had tired the sun with talk - ing and
p
15
pp
sent him down the sky. And now that thou art ly - ing, my
pp
sent him down the sky. And now that thou art ly - ing, my
pp
sent him down the sky. And now that thou art ly - ing, my
pp
sent him down the sky. And now that thou art ly - ing, my
19
dear old Ca - rian guest, A hand - ful of grey ash - es, long,
dear old Ca - rian guest, A hand - ful of grey ash - es, long,
dear old Ca - rian guest, A hand - ful of grey ash - es, long,
dear old Ca - rian guest, A hand - ful of grey ash - es, long,

23
mf
poco cresc.
long a - go at rest, Still are thy plea - sant voi - ces, Thy
pp
poco cresc.
long a - go at rest, Still are thy voi - ces, Thy
pp
[poco cresc.]
long a - go at rest, Still are thy voi - ces, Thy
pp
long a - go at rest, at
27
f
night - in - gales, a - wake, For Death, he ta - keth all a - way,
f
night - in - gales, a - wake, For Death, he ta - keth all a -
f
night - in - gales, a - wake, For Death, he ta - keth all a -
f
rest, For Death, he ta - keth all a -
31
p
pp
but them he can - not take.
p
pp
- way, but them he can - take.
p
pp
- way, but them he can - not take.
p
pp
- way, but them he can - not take.

24. The blue bird

MARY COLERIDGE

CHARLES VILLIERS STANFORD
Op. 119 No. 3

14
A bird whose wings were pa - lest
still, there flew A bird whose wings were pa - lest
still, there flew A bird whose wings were pa - lest
still, there flew A bird whose wings were pa - lest
19
ppp
blue.
p
The sky a - bove was blue at last,
cresc.
blue. The sky a - bove was blue last,
blue. The sky a - bove was blue at last,
24
p
blue,
mf
blue.
The sky be - neath me blue in blue, was
The sky be - neath me blue in blue, was
The sky be - neath me blue in blue, was

29
A mo-ment, ere the bird had passed, It caught
blue in blue, blue in blue, It
34
his im - - age, his im - age as he
caught, it caught his im - age, his im - age as he
caught, it caught his im - age as he
39
più lento
flew.
quasi niente ppp
blue.
The lake lay blue be - low the hill.

25. My love dwelt in a Northern land

ROMANCE

* The passages of vocal accompaniment to be sung as softly and smoothly as possible and without accent.

23
Wax great and white o'er wood and lawn,
watch'd the moon Wax great and white o'er wood and lawn, wax great and white o'er
Wax great and white o'er wood and lawn,
watch'd the moon Wax great and white o'er wood and lawn, wax great and white o'er
watch'd the moon Wax great and white o'er wood and lawn, wax great and white o'er
watch'd the moon Wax great o'er
27
mf dim. p pp
And oft, that month, we watch'd the moon Wax
wood and lawn, And oft, that month, we watch'd the moon, and
And oft, that month, we watch'd the moon, and
wood and lawn, And oft, that month, we watch'd the moon, and
wood and lawn, And oft, that month, we watch'd, we watch'd the
wood and lawn, And oft, that month, we watch'd, we watch'd the

32
pp
great
and
ppp
oft, that month, we watch'd the moon Wax great and white o'er
pp
oft, that month, we watch'd the moon Wax great and
ppp
oft, that month, we watch'd the moon Wax great and white o'er
ppp
moon
Wax great and white o'er
ppp
moon
Wax great
35
white o'er wood and lawn, And
wood and lawn, wax great and white o'er wood and lawn, And
white o'er wood and lawn, And
wood and lawn, wax great and white o'er wood and lawn, And
wood and lawn, wax great and white o'er wood and lawn, And
and white o'er wood and lawn,

38
wane, with wan - ing of the June,
wane, with wan - ing of the June, and wane, with wan - ing
wane, with wan - ing of the June,
wane, with wan - ing of the June, and wane, with wan - ing
wane, with wan - ing of the June, and wane, with wan - ing
And wane, with
41
f
sf
dim.
rit.
Till, like a brand for bat - tle drawn, She fell,
of the June, Till, like a brand for bat - tle drawn, She fell,
Till, like a brand for bat - tle drawn, She fell,
of the June, Till, like a brand for bat - tle drawn, She fell,
of the June, Till, like a brand for bat - tle drawn, She fell,
wan - ing June, Till, like a brand for bat - tle drawn, She fell,

45
a tempo, poco lento
rall.
she fell, and flamed in a wild dawn.
fell, she fell, and flamed in a wild dawn.
fell, she fell, and flamed in a wild dawn.
fell, she fell, and flamed in a wild dawn.
fell, she fell, and flamed in a wild dawn, in a wild dawn.
fell, she fell, and flamed in a wild dawn, in a wild dawn.
Tempo primo
legato 50
S.
A.
T.
B.
I know not if the for - est green Still gir - dles round that cas - tle
I know not if the for - est green Still gir - dles round that cas - tle
I know not if the for - est green Still gir - dles round that cas - tle
I know not if the for - est green Still gir - dles round that cas - tle
53
rit.
a tempo
gray, I know not if the boughs be - tween The white deer
gray, I know not if the boughs be - tween The white deer
gray, I know not if The white deer
gray, I know not if The white deer

56
dim.
pp
molto espress.
vanish ere the day: The grass above my
vanish ere the day: The grass above my love is green, the
60
poco rit.
a tempo, più lento
ffz p
love is green, His heart is colder than the clay,
grass above my love is green, His heart is colder than the clay,
heart is cold, colder than the
mezza voce
65
molto rall.
ppp
colder, colder than the clay.
clay, his heart is colder, colder than the clay.
than the clay.

26. As torrents in summer

HENRY LONGFELLOW

EDWARD ELGAR

12
mf
rain, for rain has been fall - ing,
mf
rain, for rain has been fall - ing,
cresc.
for rain has been fall - ing,
16
espress.
pp
pp
poco rit.
fall - ing Far off at their foun - tains;
pp
pp
rain has been fall - ing Far off at their foun - tains;
pp
pp
rain has been fall - ing Far off at their foun - tains;
pp
pp
For rain has been fall - ing at their foun - tains;
a tempo
mf
21
ten.
cresc.
So hearts that are faint - ing Grow full to o'er - flow - ing, And they that be - hold it,
mf
ten.
cresc.
So hearts that are faint - ing Grow full to o'er - flow - ing, And they that be - hold it,
mf
ten.
cresc.
So hearts that are faint - ing Grow full to o'er - flow - ing, And they that be - hold it,
mf
ten.
cresc.
So hearts that are faint - ing Grow full to o'er - flow - ing, And they that be - hold it,

26
3
f
dim.
p
they that be-hold it Mar - vel, and know_ not, mar - vel, and know not
they that be-hold it Mar - vel, and know not, mar - vel, and know not
they that be - hold it Mar - vel, mar - vel, and know not That
they that be-hold it Mar - vel, and know not, mar - vel, and know not
31
mf
dim.
cresc.
pp
That God, that God at their foun - tains, their foun - tains
That God, that God at their foun - tains, Far off has been
God, that God at their foun - tains, Far off has been
Far
37
espress.
poco rit.
pp
Far off, far off has been rain - ing!
rain - ing, far off, far off has been rain - ing!
rain - ing, far off, far off has been rain - ing!
off, far off, far off has been rain - ing!

27. Go, song of mine

GUIDO CAVALCANTI
tr. D. G. ROSETTI

EDWARD ELGAR
Op. 57

6
ppp
Go, song of mine,
ppp
Go, song of mine,
ppp
Go, song of mine,
quasi recit. molto espress.
p
Go, song of mine, To break the hard - ness of the heart of
pp
dim.
quasi recit. molto espress.
p
Go, song of mine, To break the hard - ness of the heart of
pp
dim.
ppp
Go, song of mine,
9
a tempo
pp
Say how his life be -
cresc.
pp
Say how his life be -
cresc.
pp
Say how his life be -
cresc.
man:
p
Say how his life be -
cresc.
man:
p
Say how his life be -
cresc.
[pp]
Say how his life be -
cresc.

allargando
dim. molto
- gan From dust, and in that dust, that dust doth sink su - pine:
rit.
Go, song of mine,
quasi recit. molto espress.
distinto, dim. e rit.
Say how his life be - gan, From dust, and in that dust doth sink su - pine:

a tempo
Molto sostenuto e cantabile
19
p
cresc.
sf ten.
sf
Yet, say, yet, say, th'un - err - ing spi - rit of grief shall
Yet, say, yet, say, th'un - err - ing spi - rit of grief
Yet, say, yet, say, th'un - err - ing spi - rit of grief
Yet, say, th'un - err - ing spi - rit of grief shall
Yet, say, th'un - err - ing spi - rit of grief shall
Yet, say, yet, say, th'un - err - ing spi - rit of
22
allargando
ff
guide his soul, shall guide, shall guide his soul, Yet, say, th'un-err - ing
shall guide, shall guide his soul, say, Yet, say, th'un-err - ing
shall guide, shall guide his soul, say, Yet, say, th'un-err - ing
guide His soul, shall guide, shall guide his soul, Yet, say, th'un-err - ing
guide His soul, shall guide, shall guide his soul, Yet, say, th'un-err - ing
grief shall guide, shall guide his soul, Yet, say, the un - err - ing

26
allargando
espress.
p
cresc.
f
spi - rit of grief shall guide his soul, shall guide his soul, be - ing
spi - rit of grief shall guide, shall guide his soul, shall guide his soul,
spi - rit of grief shall guide, shall guide his soul, shall guide his soul, be - ing
spi - rit of grief shall guide his soul, shall guide his soul, be - ing pu - ri - fied,
spi - rit of grief shall guide his soul, shall guide his soul, be - ing pu - ri - fied,
spi rit of grief shall guide, shall guide, guide his soul,
30
legato
ff
pu - ri - fi - ed, pu - ri - fi - ed, To
grief shall guide his soul, be - ing pu - ri - fi - ed, be - ing
pu - ri - fi - ed, pu - ri - fi - ed, be - ing
grief shall guide his soul, be - ing pu - ri - fi - ed,
grief shall guide his soul, be - ing pu - ri - fi - ed,
be - ing pu - ri - fi - ed, pu - ri - fi - ed, be - ing
be - ing pu - ri - fi - ed, be - ing

34
rf
ten.
fff
seek its Ma - ker at the heav'n - - - - - -
pu - ri - fied, pu - ri - fied, To seek its Ma - ker at the
pu - ri - fied, pu - ri - fied, To seek its Ma - ker at the
pu - ri - fi - ed, To seek its Ma - ker at the
pu - ri - fied, pu - ri - fied, To seek its Ma - ker at the
pu - ri - fi - ed, To seek its Ma - ker at the
pu - ri - fi - ed, To seek its Ma - ker at the
37
sf
- - - ly, heav'n - - - - - - - - - ly
heav'n - ly shrine, to seek its Ma - ker at the heav'n - ly shrine, to
heav'n - ly shrine, to seek its Ma - ker at the heav'n - ly shrine, to
heav'n - ly shrine, to seek its Ma - ker at the heav'n - ly shrine, to
heav'n - ly shrine, to seek its Ma - ker at the heav'n - ly shrine, to
heav'n - ly shrine, to seek its Ma - ker at the heav'n - ly shrine, to
heav'n - ly shrine, to seek its Ma - ker at the heav'n - ly shrine, to

40
dim.
p
shrine; His soul, be - ing
sf
dim.
p
seek its Ma - ker at the heav'n - ly shrine; The un - err - ing
sf
dim.
p
seek its Ma - ker at the heav'n - ly shrine; The un - err - ing
sf
dim.
p
seek its Ma - ker at the heav'n - ly shrine; Th' un - err - ing
sf
dim.
p
seek its Ma - ker at the heav'n - ly shrine; The un - err - ing
dim.
seek its Ma - ker at the heav'n - ly shrine,
dim.
p
seek its Ma - ker at the heav'n - ly shrine,
43
più lento
pp
molto espress.
p
pu - ri - fied, shall seek its Ma - ker at the
pp
molto espress.
p
spi - rit of grief shall guide His soul to its Ma - ker at the
pp
molto espress.
p
spi - rit of grief shall guide His soul to its Ma - ker at the
pp
molto espress.
p
spi - rit of grief shall guide His soul to its Ma - ker at the
pp
molto espress.
p
spi - rit of grief shall guide His soul to its Ma - ker at the
p
pp
to seek, to seek its Ma - ker,
pp
to seek, to seek its Ma -

46
dolcissimo
dim. molto
pp
heav'n - ly shrine, at the heav'n - ly shrine.
heav'n - ly shrine, pu - ri - fied, at the heav'n - ly
heav'n - ly shrine, pu - ri - fied, at the heav'n - ly
heav'n - ly shrine, at the heav'n - ly, heav'n - ly
heav'n - ly shrine, at the heav'n - ly, heav'n - ly
pu - ri - fi - ed, pu - ri - fi - ed.
- ker, pu - ri - fi - ed.
50
lunga
Come prima
p
In tears, go, song of mine, To break the
shrine. In tears, go, song of mine, To break the
shrine. In tears, go, song of mine, To break the
shrine. In tears, go, song of mine, To break the
shrine. In tears, go, song of mine, To break the
In tears, go, song of mine, To break the

53

p *ppp*
hard - ness of the heart ___ of man: ___ Go, ___

p *ppp*
hard - ness of the heart ___ of man: ___ Go, ___

p *ppp*
hard - ness of the heart ___ of man: ___ Go, ___

p *quasi recit. molto espress.* *pp*
hard - ness of the heart of man: Go, song of mine, To

p *quasi recit. molto espress.* *pp*
hard - ness of the heart of man: Go, song of mine, To

p *ppp*
hard - ness of the heart of man: ___ Go,

57

pp
song of mine, ___ Go!

pp
___ song ___ of mine, ___ Go!

pp
___ song ___ of mine, ___ Go!

pp *dim.*
break ___ the hard - ness ___ of the heart of man. ___

pp *dim.*
break ___ the hard - ness ___ of the heart of man. ___

pp
song of mine, ___ Go!

28. Full fathom five

WILLIAM SHAKESPEARE

CHARLES WOOD

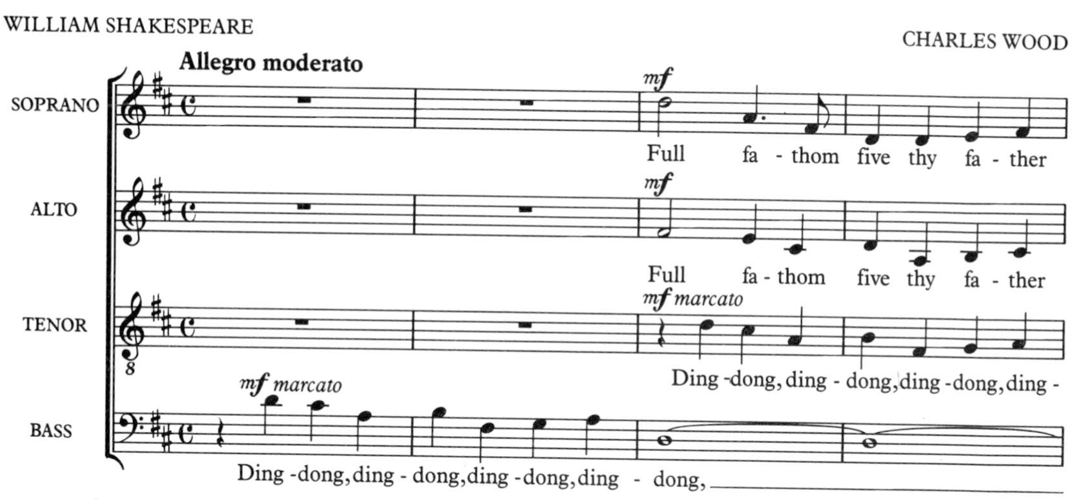

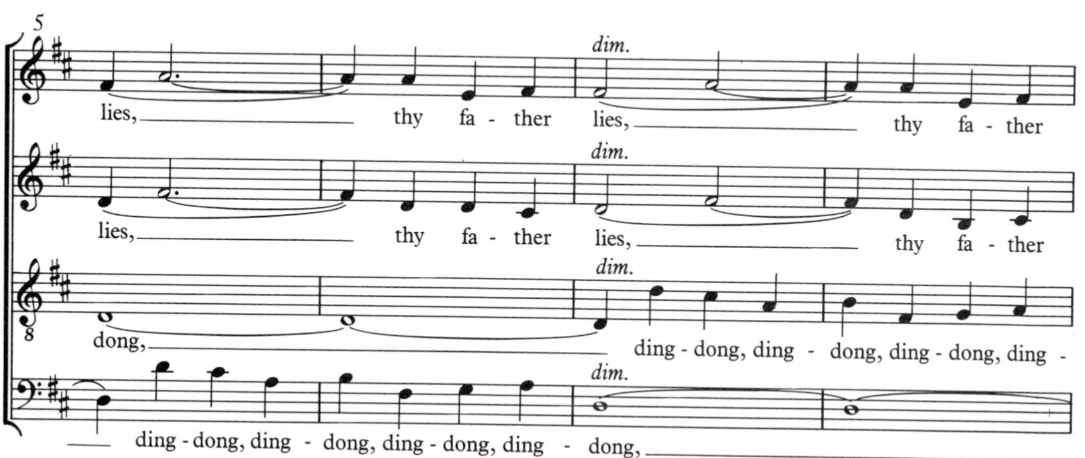

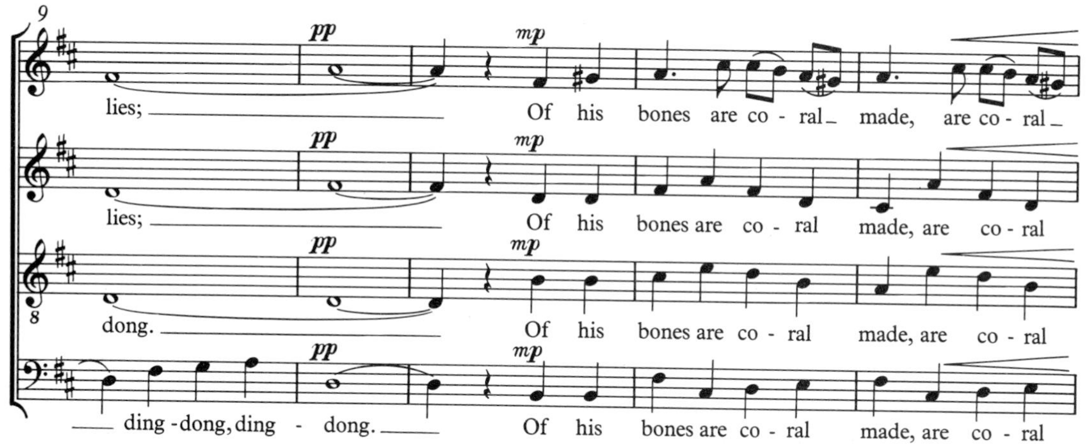

14
f dim. p
made; Those are pearls that were his
f marcato dim. p
made; Ding - dong, ding - dong, ding - dong, ding - dong. Those are pearls that were his
f dim. p
made, are co - ral made; Those are pearls that were
f dim. p
made; Those are pearls that were his
18
cresc.
eyes, are pearls that were his eyes; No - thing of him
cresc.
eyes, are pearls that were his eyes; No - thing of him
cresc.
his eyes, are pearls that were his eyes; No - thing of him
cresc.
eyes, are pearls that were his eyes; No - thing of him
23
f p cresc. f
that doth fade, But doth suf - fer a sea - change In - to
f p cresc. f
that doth fade, But doth suf - fer a sea - change In - to
f p cresc. f
that doth fade, But doth suf - fer a sea - change In - to
f p cresc. f
that doth fade, But doth suf - fer a sea-change In - -

28
some - thing rich and strange, in - to some - thing rich and
some - thing rich and strange, in - to some - thing rich and
some - thing rich and strange, in - to some - thing rich and
- - to some - thing rich and
33
dim.
strange.
p
f
Sea - nymphs
dim.
strange.
p
Ding - dong, ding - dong.
f
dim.
strange.
p
f marcato
Ding-dong, ding -
dim.
strange. Ding - dong, ding - dong, ding - dong, ding - dong, ding - dong, ding - dong,
p
f
37
hour - ly ring his knell, sea - nymphs
Sea - nymphs, sea - nymphs
dong, ding - dong, ding - dong, ding - dong, ding -
marcato
ding - dong, ding - dong, ding - dong, ding - dong,

41
p
hour - ly ring his knell, Hark! now I
hour - ly ring his knell, Hark! now I
dong, ding - dong, ding - dong. Hark! now I
ding - dong, ding - dong, ding - dong, ding - dong, ding - dong, ding -
45
cresc.
hear them, hark! now I hear them, Ding - dong,
hear them, hark! now I hear them,
hear them, hark! now I hear them, Ding - dong, ding -
dong, ding - dong, ding - dong, ding - dong, ding - dong, ding - dong bell,
ding - dong bell.
49
rall.
f
ff
ding - dong bell, ding - dong bell.
Ding - dong, ding - dong bell.
Ding - dong, ding - dong, ding - dong bell.
dong, ding - dong, ding - dong bell.
ding - dong, ding - dong, ding, ding - dong bell.

29. Oh where art thou dreaming?

THOMAS MOORE

HAMISH MACCUNN

13
poco rall.
f
dim.
p
dim.
home, And the night is fast go - ing, But thou art not come,
home, And the night is fast go - ing, But thou art not come,
home, And the night is fast go - ing, But thou art not come,
home, And the night is fast go - ing, But thou art not come,
18
[a tempo]
pp
mf
No, thou com - - est not. 'Tis the
No, thou com - - est not. 'Tis the
No, thou com - - est not. 'Tis the
No, thou com - - est not. 'Tis the time
23
time when night flo - wers Should wake from their rest, 'Tis the
time when night flo - wers Should wake from their rest, 'Tis the
time when night flo - wers Should wake from their rest, 'Tis the
when night flo - wers Should wake from their rest, 'Tis the

27
hour of all hours When the lute sing - eth best; But the
hour of all hours When the lute sing - eth best; But the
hour of all hours When the lute sing - eth best; But the
hour of all hours When the lute sing - eth best; But the
31
cresc.
f
dim.
flowers are half sleep - ing Till thy glance they see, And the
flowers are half sleep - ing Till thy glance they see, And the
flowers are half sleep - ing Till thy glance they see, And the
flowers are half sleep - ing Till thy glance they see, And the
35
p
poco rall.
dim.
a tempo
pp
hushed lute is keep - ing Its mu - sic for thee, Yet thou
hushed lute is keep - ing Its mu - sic for thee, Yet thou
hushed lute is keep - ing Its mu - sic for thee, Yet thou
hushed lute is keep - ing Its mu - sic for thee, Yet thou

40
com - est not, thou com - - - - -
com - est not, thou com - - - - -
com - est not, Oh where art thou dream - ing, On
com - est not, thou com - - - - - - - - - - -
espress.
46
meno mosso
poco rall.
- - - est not. In my lat - tice is gleam - ing The
- - - est not. In my lat - tice is gleam - ing The
land or on sea? In my lat - tice is gleam - ing The
- - - est not, thou com - - - - - - -
dim.
51
Adagio
watch - light for thee, the watch - light for thee.
watch - light for thee, the watch - light for thee.
watch - light for thee, the watch - light for thee.
- - - est not, thou com - est not.

30. Summer is gone

CHRISTINA ROSSETTI

S. COLERIDGE-TAYLOR

poco rit.
13
e - ven Au - tumn clo - ses, and Au - tumn clo - ses, and
e - ven Au - tumn clo - ses, and
e - ven Au - tumn clo - ses, and
e - ven Au - tumn clo - ses, and
16
pp
Au - tumn clo - - - - ses.
Au - tumn clo - ses, and Au - tumn clo - ses.
Au - tumn clo - ses, and Au - tumn clo - ses.
e - ven Au - tumn clo - ses, and Au - tumn clo - ses.
21
a tempo
fp
Yea! Au - tumn's chil - ly self is go - ing, And
Yea! Au - tumn's chil - ly self is go - ing, And
Yea! Au - tumn's chil - ly self is go - ing, And
Yea! Au - tumn's chil - ly self is go - ing, And

25
win - ter comes which is yet cold - er, Each
win - ter comes which is yet cold - er, Each
win - ter comes which is yet cold - er, Each
win - ter comes which is yet cold - er, Each
29
day the hoar - frost wax - es bold - er, And the
day the hoar - frost wax - es bold - er, And the
day the hoar - frost wax - es bold - er, And the
day the hoar - frost wax - es bold - er, And the
poco rall.
33
last buds cease blow - ing, the last buds cease blow - ing,
last buds cease blow - ing, the last buds cease blow - ing, the
last buds cease blow - ing, the last buds cease blow - ing, the
last buds cease blow - ing, the last buds cease blow - ing, the

Printed in Great Britain by Alden Press Ltd., Oxford